THE LAND OF NIGHTMARES

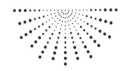

DAVID PURSE

inked entertainment

To Cathie-Mae. Dream big, kiddo!

1

MS. GLOOMBERG'S HOME FOR
WAYWARD CHILDREN

*M*ona sat in the back of the police car and glared at Officer Joe's bald head.

He turned in his seat and faced her. "Now Mona, you promised me I wouldn't have to pick you up again."

"I didn't plan on you catching me this time," she grumbled, folding her arms.

Joe sighed and started the engine, taking the all-too-familiar route back to the very place Mona was trying to get away from.

Mona stared out the window. Lights flickered on along the city streets as darkness crept in, chasing people eager to get home and out of the rain.

At least they had homes to go to.

Mona had been so close this time—bought a train

1

ticket and everything. She crumpled the now-useless ticket to freedom in her hand and tossed it against the glass partition separating the front of the car from the back.

Before long, Officer Joe pulled up to the sidewalk and parked the car. He got out and opened her door, like he was a limo driver and she was a young starlet ready to walk the red carpet and pose for the paparazzi.

Yeah, right. All Mona had waiting on her was a royally ticked-off Ms. Gloomberg who stood by the front door of the old brownstone, posture rigid and clothes better suited for someone's funeral.

Mona was so dead.

Officer Joe spoke with Ms. Gloomberg for a moment and then returned to his car, waving Mona off as he sped down the street and left her to face the wrath of the old woman.

The rain soaked through Mona's ragged hand-me-down sweater, but she took her time ascending the stone steps, delaying the inevitable for as long as possible.

"Get inside," hissed Ms. Gloomberg, ushering Mona in with a firm grip on her shoulder.

The door slammed behind them as thunder roared outside. Ms. Gloomberg marched straight through the hallway to her office, clicking her fingers at Mona to follow.

Whispers came from upstairs as a bunch of faces peered down from over the rail of the rickety staircase, kids shoving each other out of the way for a better look.

"Is it a new kid?"

"Nah, it's just Mona."

"I thought she was placed with a family?"

"She was."

Mona dragged her feet, sodden sneakers squishing with every step. She entered the office and scrunched her nose as the aroma of cat hair and too much lavender perfume assaulted her senses.

Mona slumped into the chair facing the desk. Her body shivered as the cold seeped through her skin and chilled her to the bone.

Ms. Gloomberg rummaged inside an old filing cabinet and hoisted out Mona's case file. The over-stuffed manila folder fell with a thump onto the oak desk, four times as big as any of the other orphans living there. Pages escaped and covered the uncarpeted floor.

The director of the "group home" took her seat, found an empty page at the back of the case file, and began scratching in Mona's latest indiscretion with angered scribbles of red ink.

Ms. Gloomberg didn't do computers. Anything invented after the abacus was deemed too high tech and something only "kids these days" wasted their time with.

When she finished, Ms. Gloomberg closed the file and rested clenched hands over it.

"What am I going to do with you?" she said, tutting as she shook her head, gray hair unmoving in its severe bun.

Mona didn't respond. A clock ticked in the background as rain rattled against the window looking out to the concrete-covered garden beyond.

"The Carsons called me worried sick about you," said Ms. Gloomberg, face as sour as winter lemons.

Mona sat up straight and raised her chin. "The Carsons don't want me."

"Can you blame them after the amount of trouble and stress you've put them through?"

"I didn't fit in there."

"Like you didn't fit in with the last family? Or the one before that? It doesn't seem like you fit in anywhere. How do you expect to be adopted if you continually prove yourself a problem?"

Mona huffed. "Who says I want to be adopted?"

A funny look crossed Ms. Gloomberg's face. "All orphans do."

"Not this one."

"Liar. One of the many attributes that will see you back here time and time again if you do not change your ways." Ms. Gloomberg stared at Mona, eyes hard. "You will be placed with a new family tomorrow. I want you up and ready first thing."

Mona sprang from her seat. "Tomorrow? Placements take at least a week."

"I'm not keeping you any longer than I have to," said Ms. Gloomberg, moving Mona's folder away to the edge of her desk.

Not another family. Not another place where she didn't belong. At least in the orphanage she was around other kids like her. Mona balled her shaking hands, nails digging into her palms.

"I can't go to another foster family," she said, trying to keep her voice level. "My parents will be back for me soon; they've just been really busy working undercover for the government."

Ms. Gloomberg frowned. "You and I both know that isn't true."

Mona slammed her fists on the desk. "But these new people aren't my family."

"You don't have a family," Ms. Gloomberg snapped. Lightning split the sky outside and lit up the room. "You will go to your new placement tomorrow, and if you run away again, you won't be coming back here. You can be someone else's problem. Now march straight upstairs and go to bed, you insolent girl."

Ms. Gloomberg went back to her paperwork and ignored Mona like she wasn't there. Mona's shoulders fell.

"Please don't send me away. I'll be good, I swear."

No reply.

"Fine," Mona spat. "I hate it here anyway." She marched straight out the office, slamming the door as hard as she could. Mona kicked the wood with the heel of her shoe and screamed.

Her voice echoed down the empty corridor as she fought back tears, swiping her face with the back of her hand. The urge to run away burned inside her, but it was no use. All her money was gone, wasted on the train ticket she never got to use.

Every part of her body ached from the cold, fatigue seeping deep into her muscles. She trudged upstairs, the old, rotting floorboards complaining at her with each step.

"Leave me alone," said a familiar voice from above.

"Give me your money and I will," said another.

Mona quickened her pace and reached the top of the stairs to find a blond eight-year-old pinned against the wall by an overgrown chump who needed to be taken down a peg or two.

Mona pinched the bridge of her nose. Today had

been a long day, and her bed called to her. Better make it quick.

Two strides later and Mona was right behind the great oaf. She grabbed the baseball bat he held in his meaty fist and yanked it from his grasp. She twirled it in her hand and jabbed him in the stomach, causing him to yelp.

"Why don't you pick on someone your own size, George?" said Mona, stretching her neck to glare up at him. Ally was easy pickings for George. No way would he ever try it with one of the bigger kids. Or her.

"What the hell, Mona?" he said, rubbing where she'd hit him.

"Shut up." Mona turned her attention to the girl. "Ally, you okay?"

Ally nodded.

George grabbed for his bat, but Mona saw it coming and stepped to the side. He stumbled over his big feet and tripped, landing hard on the ground. Mona stood over him and held the bat to his nose.

"Next time I catch you picking on her, I'm going to pretend your head is a ball and hit a home run. Understand?"

George edged away and got to his feet. He turned to leave but then hovered at a safe distance.

Mona groaned. "What?"

"My bat," he said, putting his hand out for it.

Mona shrugged. "It's mine now."

George began to protest, but he took another step back when Mona raised the bat and rested it on her shoulder. He scuttled away into his room without another word.

"Thanks, Mona," said Ally, speaking up now that George was gone. "He was trying to take my money. I have three whole dollars."

Mona walked over to her and rested a hand on her tiny shoulder. "You need to learn to stick up for yourself. No one else will."

Ally wasn't cut out for this place. The other kids would eat her up once they discovered Ms. Gloomberg was washing her hands of Mona.

"I know," Ally said, looking at her feet.

"Let's go to bed. It's past curfew and we don't want Ms. Gloomberg catching us tonight, believe me."

They made their way down the hall and entered the bedroom they shared. There hadn't been a new girl during Mona's absence, so her bed was still hers.

She crossed the room to the closet with no door on it and changed out of her wet clothes into dry ones, relishing an oversized hoodie she had claimed from one of the boxes of clothes people sometimes sent over. It fell to her knees, but it would heat her up in no time.

"How far did you get this time?" asked Ally, who changed into pink polka-dot pajamas.

"Not far enough," Mona replied. "I'm being placed with new strangers tomorrow."

Mona lost count of the number of foster families she'd had. They were all the same, though, the same cycle repeating over and over again. Things would be fine for the first couple of days and then they wouldn't be. Each time they blamed Mona, and most of the time they were right. Trouble had a way of finding her.

A small bookshelf sat near her bed and she ran a hand over her few belongings. She never bothered to take anything with her when sent to a family. She was never there long enough to miss them.

A pile of well-loved books sat next to Mr. Gordo, a teddy bear she used to carry everywhere when she was younger. He was missing an eye, and Mona no longer needed him to make her feel safe, but she couldn't face throwing him out. She wouldn't make him an orphan too.

"Maybe this time it'll be different," said Ally. "Maybe they'll be kind and love you and you'll get adopted."

"Maybe," said Mona, forcing a smile. She went to the other bed and tucked Ally in. "Get some sleep."

"Night, Mona."

Mona kissed her forehead. "Don't let the bedbugs bite."

Ally closed her eyes and the room grew quiet, the storm outside the only thing keeping Mona company.

She crossed the room and sat on the window ledge, hugging her knees. The moon looked down at her and shined through the window like an ever-watchful night-light. The city lay under it, buildings reaching for the sky and twinkling like stars.

Ally's light snores filled the room a few minutes later. She would get adopted soon. Ally was exactly what prospective parents looked for: young, cute, quiet, and white.

Mona was none of those things.

At this point, her future was pretty much mapped out. She'd seen it happen to the older kids, the ones no one wanted. Trapped in the system, hopping from place to place until the day she turned eighteen when she would no longer be a burden to the state, booted out to take care of herself.

Mona gripped the curtain.

She didn't need a perfect new family. She didn't need anybody.

She'd been all she needed since as long as she could remember, since the first day she arrived at Ms. Gloomberg's after her mom died, her dad unfit to look after her because he loved his drugs more than he did Mona. He'd visited a couple times during those early days, then vanished off the face of the earth. He could be dead too for all she knew.

No, she didn't need anybody. If no one wanted her, then she didn't want them either. She'd make it on her own.

Gray, angry clouds passed over the moon, blocking the night sky, but Mona's head was clear as a summer's day.

A social worker would arrive tomorrow morning to take her to a new family, but Mona had no intentions of being there. If what she had in mind worked, she'd be long gone by then.

Mona got up and stuffed some clothes into a backpack, along with a few of her books and Mr. Gordo. She shrugged on a rainproof jacket and sat it by her bed for when the time came.

The old alarm clock beside her bed still worked, and she set it for three in the morning. It was Mona's best and only shot to escape unnoticed. Everyone would be asleep by then, even Ms. Gloomberg who stayed up late to read the cheesy romance books she kept hidden in her drawer with men in kilts on the cover.

Before she left, she would wake up Ally and tell her she was going. It would be hard to leave Ally for good and say goodbye, but Mona's mind was made up.

Keeping her outdoor clothes on, she slipped into

bed and stared at the ceiling. Multicolored stars were drawn above her, done in crayon by Ally with smiley faces. She'd drawn them for her after Mona complained you couldn't see the stars in the city.

The tears she willed away earlier returned, and in the stillness of the night, Mona allowed them to fall.

Mona learned long ago that dreams never came true, but as she lay there, she wished on the crayon stars with all her might to be anywhere but the orphanage or with a foster family. She wanted it more than anything. There had to be something better out there for her than this. Somewhere far, far away. There just had to be.

After a while, Mona fell into a dreamless sleep.

A strange noise roused her sometime later that night. Rubbing her eyes, Mona sat up on her bed and peered through the darkness.

A gust of wind swept through the bedroom and brushed past her face. It slapped her awake with a panicked jolt as she lay eyes on what the noise was.

Not what. Who.

Someone was opening the bedroom window.

From the outside.

2

AN INTRUDER IN THE NIGHT

A figure slipped in through the window.

Mona jumped out of bed and snatched George's baseball bat, raising it high, ready to swing. She screwed her eyes to get a better look, but it was too dark. Everything was shrouded in shadow.

Thunder clapped outside.

Howling wind blew the curtains in the air. They rattled against the restraint of their hooks, flapping with loud snaps as the bitter cold invaded the room.

Lightning struck and illuminated inside.

Mona saw the flash of a face, the angles harsh in the sudden burst of light. It was gone in an instant and Mona's vision blurred. She stepped away and her back hit the wall. The intruder still lingered in the dark; she could sense him.

Taking her bat, she swung blindly in front of her and hit nothing but air. Her heart drummed in her ear, legs shaking under her. She reached for Ally but tripped and fell over her blanket that draped over the floor.

Frantic, Mona rolled and tried to get up, only to tangle herself in the sheets. She got ready to scream at the top of her lungs and wake up the whole house for help when suddenly, the lights came on.

Mona wriggled free from the blanket and jumped to her feet. A man stood near the bedroom door, blocking her exit.

"Ah, good. You're already dressed," he said.

He was rather short, only a head taller than Mona. Old too, with more lines on his face than the city subway system. Silver hair was cropped at the sides of his head together with a pair of bushy eyebrows and a long beard in the same shade.

Mona frowned at his odd clothes. Instead of a shirt and trousers, he wore a luxurious-looking pair of pajamas in a rich, midnight purple, laced with gold thread depicting a galaxy of stars across his draping housecoat. A crescent moon was embroidered on each of his slippers in matching colors, the tips curling up at the toes.

He even had a hat, a strange, pointy thing that flopped to the side.

The intruder didn't scream *danger* to Mona, but looks could be deceiving, and he hadn't crawled through her window in the middle of the night to say hi.

"What do you want?" Mona asked, putting herself between the man and Ally, who slept through all the commotion.

"I'm here to see Mona," he said in a regal British accent.

Mona tightened her grip on the bat. "What do you want with her?"

"Oh, I'm dreadfully sorry. I thought you were her. I must have gotten the wrong room." He reached for the door handle, muttering to himself.

Mona should have let him go, should have allowed him to put as much distance between them as possible so she could run and get help, but there was something about him. He gave off a weird vibe, a silent, calming presence. Interest got the better of her. "I'm Mona. Who are you?"

"I'm the Sandman."

"The Sandman?" Mona laughed. "Okay, Grandpa, and I'm Easter Bunny."

The guy had probably wandered out of the nursing home a couple blocks away. Her tense muscles relaxed a little. He wasn't there for some sinister reason; he was just lost and delusional. Poor dude. His caregivers would be out looking for him, along with Officer Joe and the rest of the precinct.

Behind her, Ally moaned in her sleep and tossed around. Her eyes began to pry open when the old man took something from a pouch and threw it over her. It glittered in the night and swirled above Ally's head.

"Hey, what the heck—"

Mona stopped what was about to be a tirade of choice words as the rainbow-colored sand gathered together. The clusters morphed into shapes, odd and distorted at first. They twirled in the air and within seconds, they took form.

From the sand materialized the silhouettes of three dolphins and a little girl. They solidified and one of the dolphins let out a happy whistle as it leaped above the others.

Mona watched the sparkling miniature animals in awe.

The sand girl became clear and more distinct. It was a tiny version of Ally. Sand-Ally splashed around in water Mona couldn't see and held on to one of the dolphins who swam her around and around in circles on its back. She giggled out loud with glee, happier than Mona had ever seen her.

A contented sigh left the real Ally's lips as the sand danced above her while she slept.

Mona glanced between Ally and the old man

several times, her brain trying to catch up with what she'd just witnessed. She moved closer to the sand figures and stared in wonder, reaching out with her hand. They looked so real.

One of the dolphins nudged her finger with a playful snout.

Mona gasped and smiled. "You really are the Sandman."

"Yes," he said with a twinkle in his eye.

Mona pinched herself, but this wasn't a dream. It was really happening. She ran a hand through her brown curls. Her heart fluttered in her chest and she had to close her mouth to stop her jaw from hitting the floor.

She motioned to the scene playing out above her roommate's head. "And Ally's dreaming this right now?"

The Sandman walked toward the bed and stood next to her. He chuckled as one of the dolphins squirted water all over Ally's face. "Yes, dolphins are her favorite." He pointed to the bat Mona still held, just in case. "And George dreams of being a star baseball player."

"What about me?" Mona could never remember any of her dreams when she awoke the next morning. They slipped through her memory like grains of sand.

The Sandman put an arm around her and led her to the window. "That's why I'm here."

Mona moved away from his touch. "I don't understand."

The storm was settling outside, the clouds beginning to part to allow the moon its rightful place. They stared out, watching the rain fall to the street and trickle down the drains to the bowels of the city below.

"Your dream. It's been calling to me for a while now, and it grew so loud tonight, I simply could not ignore it." His eyes grew shiny, the moon's reflection glinting off them as he looked at her with an expression she couldn't decipher.

"You hear people's dreams?" she asked. The question sounded stupid out loud. Here she was, asking the Sandman stuff. She didn't believe he, or any other people like him, even existed. Though, it was kinda hard to ignore when the guy was literally standing in her bedroom.

Of all the things Mona thought she would be doing tonight, she would never have guessed this in a million years.

Sandman averted his gaze and cleared his throat. "Of course. I don't just deal in the dreams you have when you're asleep, you know. I know the dreams you have when awake too."

Mona scratched the back of her head. "You mean,

about running away from the orphanage and foster families?"

Would he make her stay? Is that why he'd come? To talk her into remaining there and going off to another set of fake parents the next day? If it was, he was out of luck. Her mind was made up and not even the Sandman could change it. One way or another, Mona would find a way to escape.

Sandman shook his head. "Not necessarily that, though I guess the desire to run away is, in part, a reaction to what you truly dream."

"But I don't have any other dreams." Leaving the orphanage was all Mona had ever wanted.

"That's not altogether true." Sandman leaned his elbows on the sill, looking out the open window. "You see, you desire your dream to come true so much that you refuse to even acknowledge it exists in the first place."

Mona sighed at the old man's riddles. She had one dream and one dream only. "You're talking in circles. Just spit it out. Why are you here?" While it was nice to stand there and listen to Sandman babble on, she had plans to make her dream a reality tonight, and it couldn't be postponed until the next evening.

Sandman turned and clasped his hands in front of him. His lip curved with a hint of an amused grin. "Very well. I have a proposition for you."

"What?"

Sandman considered her for a second. "It's better if I show you, I think."

"So, show me."

Sandman leaned out the window and whistled. The next second, a set of rope ladders fell from above and stopped right at the foot of the window.

"I hope you don't mind climbing," he said. "Or heights."

"Yeah, right. I'm not afraid of anything." Though she wasn't stupid. "Why should I trust you?" she demanded.

"Please, by all means, stay here if you wish, but I promise that if you come with me and hear what I have to say, I will make sure you return in time for whatever you have that alarm clock set for." He gave her a knowing look with his deep blue eyes.

Mona bit her bottom lip. He might be the Sandman, but she didn't know him. She may not have been raised by her parents, but even she knew not to go off with strangers.

Then again, what did she have to stay for? All her past attempts at running away had failed. Ally would be adopted soon. Ms. Gloomberg wanted nothing more to do with Mona, and quite frankly, the feeling was mutual as far as Mona was concerned.

Maybe this was her big chance. Maybe whatever

awaited her with this mysterious man was her ticket out.

"Feel free to bring that bat of yours," added Sandman, the wind blowing his beard. He swung his legs over the windowsill and placed his feet on the ladder rungs. "If I turn out to be evil, you can whack me over the head with it."

Mona grabbed her backpack from the floor and hoisted a strap over one shoulder. She joined Sandman at the window and twirled the bat with deft hands.

"Okay, but I'm warning you, old man, I'm pretty good with this thing."

"Jolly good," said Sandman, and he began to climb.

Mona stole one last glimpse at Ally and her bedroom, and then followed the Sandman, leaving the orphanage behind her.

3
THE SANCTUARY

Mona desperately held on to the rope ladder. The wind grew stronger the higher up she went, whipping at her clothes and battering against her ears. She made the mistake of looking down. It was a long way to fall to nothing but city concrete.

"Almost there," came Sandman's muffled voice above her.

Mona strained her neck. Almost there? All she could see past Sandman was clouds and the dull night sky.

Sandman climbed a few more rungs and the next minute he vanished out of sight. Mona froze. What happened? Where did he go? Did he fall? Did the wind blow him off the ladder? His frail hands could have lost their hold.

The tips of Mona's fingers felt like icicles. "Sandman?" she called.

Her hair blew in her face as a gust whooshed past and sent the rope ladder spinning in the air. Mona screamed but it got lost in the rushing air. She clamped her eyes shut.

"I've got you," came Sandman's voice.

Mona followed the sound and Sandman's head popped out of the sky. She screamed again.

His upper half came into view next as he leaned forward and reached out for her. Mona panicked and clung to the ladder. Where was the rest of his body? Where was he taking her? He was an old man. Could he even carry her weight? Now wasn't exactly a good time to test that out given that she was hovering high above the orphanage rooftop.

"Let go," he said, taking her arms.

It was either let go or stay there swinging around at the whim of Mother Nature. Mona met his calm eyes. She loosened her death grip on the rung and pried her frozen fingers off one by one. Sandman dragged her up, stronger than he appeared.

Mona hung in the air, her stomach doing backflips.

"There we go," said Sandman, sitting her down on something solid. "You're quite safe."

Mona panted, her breathing labored as her heart tried to settle down to a riot in her chest. A varnished wooden floor lay under her. Certain she wasn't going to hurl, or fall to a splattered end, she got up on unsteady legs.

It wasn't a floor. It was a deck.

"No way," Mona whispered, taking in her surroundings. She dumped her backpack with the bat sticking out of the top and walked around.

Massive white sails hung from three huge masts that sprouted from the deck. Shrouds held them up with rope footholds to climb and stand in the crow's nest to keep watch for oncoming ships. Though Mona doubted they had to worry about that given they weren't at sea. They were more likely to come across airplanes and unsuspecting birds.

The ship was just how Mona imagined the pirate ships in her books, minus the skull-and-crossbones flags and swashbuckling pirates fighting over rum and stolen treasure. It was like something out of a dream.

"What is this place?" she asked, turning to Sandman.

Sandman waved his hand and announced, "This is the Sanctuary."

With a click of his fingers, a loud horn bellowed from somewhere near the front and the ship began to move. The sails expanded and reached out to their full length. The wind caught in them and the ship soared forward, the bowsprit like a big finger pointing in the direction they were headed.

Mona wobbled but Sandman was there to keep her steady. He led her up a set of stairs to the aft of the ship where a large wooden wheel navigated the way of its own accord.

Mona inched with careful footing to the ship's edge and leaned over. They coursed through the sky like it was a vast blue ocean, the clouds flowing out at either end of the ship upon impact in waves of sea foam.

The city slept below them, unaware of their presence high above.

"Why couldn't I see the ship from the ladders?" Mona asked.

Sandman joined her and peered down. "It is invisible, of course. I cannot fly my ship around the world for everyone to see."

"So, this is how you get around?"

"It gets me from place to place," said Sandman.

"It beats the subway, that's for sure." There wasn't a rat or questionable puddle in sight.

The ship tilted up from the bow ever so slightly and ascended higher. The horn blared again.

"Hold on to your hats," called Sandman, taking one of the hanging ropes and bracing himself for something. Mona followed suit. The Sanctuary's insides grumbled below their feet and the entire ship began to vibrate.

"Uh, Sandman, what's going—"

Boom!

The ship took off like a rocket. It soared higher and higher, straight through the clouds. Thick, wet mist swept through the deck and brushed Mona's face as the ship traveled at top speed.

Mona laughed, her stomach dropping like she was on a roller coaster. "Woohoo!"

The ship broke through the wall of murky clouds like a cannonball and shot out into one of the most beautiful sights Mona had ever seen.

The ship slowed again and righted itself to a level angle. Mona ran down the steps and across the deck to the very tip of the bow.

Real stars. Hundreds of them. Thousands. Hundreds of thousands, everywhere the eye could see. They twinkled from their perches like diamonds glittering from the ceiling of a vast and magical cave of wonders.

The bright city lights and layers of smog obliterated any chance of Mona ever seeing something like this. Now she could see a whole galaxy of stars and reveled under their majestic glory.

"Very pretty for balls of gas," commented Sandman behind her.

"I could stand here and watch them forever," said Mona.

"We could do that, though I would like to give you a tour of the place."

"What about your big proposition?" As much fun as she was having, Mona still didn't know why she was there.

"I can tell you along the way," he said, heading back to the middle of the deck. Mona tore her eyes from the stars and caught up to him, matching his steady, casual stroll.

They entered a door to the starboard side and carried on downstairs to the next deck below. The inside of the ship was large, with high ceilings and wide corridors decorated in maple wood floors, plush red rugs, and gold wallpaper with a delicate lace design. Brass pipes ran along the walls in an intricate network, rattling and whistling above them as they passed.

Sandman took a left down another corridor and reached a large door with a painted rainbow carved into it. "This is the Sand Room," he said, opening the door and motioning for Mona to go inside.

"Wow," said Mona as she entered.

The entire room glittered in bursts of radiant hues. A glow emanated from a huge waterfall of sand, covering everything with pure light, which bounced off the pristine white walls in a kaleidoscope of rainbow colors.

The sand fell from the edge of a wide chute at the top of the room, toppling down into a massive mixing bowl where a paddle stirred the sand. The bowl narrowed at the bottom in a funnel shape where sand spurted out of taps and landed into smaller bowls, each of them holding a single designated color.

Large, clear tubes carried the sand all the way down to a station of dispensers with brass handles. Below them were huge bags of sand, filled with their allocated shade of the rainbow.

Mona went to one of the bags and peered at the sparkling blue sand inside. She lowered her head to the contents and jumped back.

"I can hear it!" she exclaimed. The sand wasn't speaking to her in a language she understood exactly. It was more like their twinkling produced an understanding inside her, a warm, pleasant feeling unlike anything she'd ever felt before.

"Yes," said Sandman. "This sand is very special. It is enchanted, and if you know how to use it, you can bend it to your will and produce something magical."

"How does it work?" asked Mona, moving from one bag to the next, from red to yellow, to pink and then green.

"Each color can be used to conjure a different

element of a dream." Sandman turned the handle on one of the dispensers and glittering violet poured out. He scooped his hand under until he had a nice pile and tossed it into the air.

The sand hung in the air, defying gravity as Sandman swept his hands through it. It moved to his will, swirling into a ball. "An emotion," he said, as laughter emanated from the sand.

Sandman swiped through the sand and remolded it. "A memory."

Mona gasped as the sand formed the shape of her as a young kid, hugging her one-eyed Mr. Gordo as tightly as she could.

"A place." The sand rearranged and a replica of Ms. Gloomberg's orphanage hovered in the air.

"An object." Sandman grabbed for the sand as it assembled into a baseball bat. As his hands touched the sand, it solidified, looking like a real bat.

"And a thing." He tossed the bat into the air and it transformed into a dolphin, just like the ones he'd made for Ally. It whistled with joy and then dove into the bag of sand, bursting back into individual grains of violet.

Sandman turned off the stream of sand at the dispenser. "By combining the colors, you can piece together a complete dream and bring it to life."

Mona stood in awe. "And you give all the people in the world their dreams every night?"

"I do," he said, leading her out of his sand-sorting factory. "Among other things."

"That seems like an awful lot of work for one person," said Mona. "I mean, how can one person manage to fly around delivering dreams to everyone in the world in one night?"

"It wasn't an issue until I became the only Sand-person left."

"There were more like you?" asked Mona, taking care with each step. Walking on a moving ship took some getting used to.

"There was a team of us. Dream Weavers we were called, but they all ..." A far-off look painted Sandman's face, his lips thinning. "Well, anyway, now that I am by myself, I have to make use of good time management. Nothing a bit of help from Old Father Time can't fix."

"Old Father Time?"

"Yes, he's a grouchy old codger, but he knows a thing or two about time. Lives in a cave, can you believe it?" Sandman scoffed and shook his head. "Silly old hermit."

Mona was about to inquire further when a crash came from somewhere down the hall. They followed the noise to the port side of the ship and turned a corner into a large yet cozy kitchen.

Plates lay scattered on the floor in a broken pile, covering something under it. A head popped out from the rubble and looked around with googly eyes. It gave itself a shake, and said, "Sorry about that. I cleaned the plates extra squeaky clean and the next thing I knew, they were sliding through my hands."

"Not to worry. Accidents happen," said Sandman, helping the creature up from under the debris and dusting bits of china off his fur. "Are you all right?"

"Super," said the creature, and then his attention landed on Mona.

He was an odd creature. Around the height of Ally, he had a short, flat head hosting big, attentive eyes. His arms and legs appeared too long for his little body, and he was covered in brown and white fur, from his clawed hands to his feet and stub of a tail.

Of all the things Mona expected to see here, a talking sloth wasn't one of them.

"We have a visitor," explained Sandman.

"A visitor?" repeated the sloth with a twitch. His hair stuck out all over the place, and he looked like he had guzzled a few gallons of coffee in one go. For a sloth, he was a complete jitterbug.

"Torpid, this is Mona. Mona, this is my assistant and dear friend, Torpid."

Mona held out her hand. "Hey, nice to meet you, Torpid."

Torpid ran up to Mona and wrapped his long, fuzzy arms around her, lifting Mona right off her feet. "Oh, how nice it is to meet you."

Mona was not a hugger. She looked at Sandman for help but he just chuckled at them.

Torpid put Mona down and ran to the kitchen cabinets, grabbing things out of them and placing them on the counter. "Would you like some hot chocolate, Mona? Yes? Good. Coming right up."

There was a clatter of pans and spoons as Torpid darted around the kitchen, humming as he worked.

"Why don't we sit down," said Sandman, taking a seat at an oak breakfast table next to a large window.

Mona sat in a chair nearest the window and took in the view. The clouds weren't as bad as before, the storm seeming to have calmed down. Below, the city lights shone in a cheap imitation to the stars above them as the night went on, the sky changing a few shades lighter as morning crept in.

Torpid rummaged inside a cupboard and came scooting out with a brush, clearing away the plates. In no time, the floor was clear of broken china and he was at the table.

"Do you want marshmallows, Mona? What am I saying? Of course you want marshmallows. Ignore me.

It's almost ready," he said, going back to humming an out-of-tune song as he rushed to the stove.

"Don't mind him," whispered Sandman, hiding his mouth with a hand. "Torpid isn't used to new people. He hasn't left the Sanctuary for almost a hundred years."

"Why not?"

"He's a rather nervous sort. Gets awfully anxious when he ventures outside."

"I saw a TV show once about a woman who had agoraphobia," said Mona. "She didn't leave the house either."

Torpid arrived with three steaming mugs and sat them on the table before shuffling up on his chair. Mona's mouth watered at the chocolate aroma. "Thanks, Torpid. I've never tried this before."

"What?" said Torpid with bulging eyes.

Mona shrugged. "Ms. Gloomberg drinks it all the time before bed, but none of us are allowed to have any."

"Then drink up and enjoy while I explain why I brought you here," said Sandman, chocolate covering his top lip and moustache.

Mona giggled, not telling him, and sipped from her cup. Her taste buds exploded as hot liquid chocolate passed over her tongue. It was better than she'd imagined. She sighed and relaxed into her chair.

"As the Sandman, I have been in charge of people's dreams for a very long time now."

Mona cradled her mug in her hands, keeping them nice and warm. "Like *The Lord of the Rings* movies long, or *oh my god this school day will never end* long?"

Sandman stared at her with a confused look.

"Never mind. You were saying?"

"Uh, yes. Dream Weaving is a wonderful and very fulfilling job, and an honorable duty at that."

"I feel like there's a 'but' coming here," said Mona, taking another slurp of her chocolate.

"But, I feel the time has come for me to pass the torch to someone else."

Mona picked a marshmallow from the top of her mug and popped it in her mouth. "Why can't you keep doing it?"

Sandman took off his hat. "Well, I'm six hundred years old and I would quite like to spend my twilight years on a beach somewhere."

Mona almost spat out her drink. "Six hundred!"

Sandman ran a hand through his silver hair. "Hard to believe, I know. I don't look a day over three hundred and fifty."

And Mona thought Ms. Gloomberg was old. Yikes.

"Okay, so you want to retire," she said, sitting forward. "Where do I come into all of this?"

Sandman drained the rest of his drink. "I need an

apprentice, someone I can train to take over when the time is right and they are ready."

"Wait," said Mona. "You want me to be your apprentice?"

"Yes."

"Oh boy," said Torpid, jumping off his chair. "An apprentice. How exciting. There's so much to do. So much to prepare. I'll go and set up a bedroom for you, Mona." Torpid gulped down his hot chocolate and sped out of the kitchen, yammering to himself the whole way.

Mona regarded Sandman. "I don't know anything about dreams or magic sand. No offense, but I didn't even believe you existed until a couple hours ago."

"You do not require any prior knowledge of the art of Dream Weaving. I will instill that during your training," Sandman assured her.

Mona worried at her lip. "But I can't be your apprentice."

"Do you not wish to learn?" asked Sandman, his pleasant smile dipping. "I completely understand if you would rather not, of course."

Mona pushed her mug away. "It's not that. All of this sounds amazing, but I can't do your job. I can't even go a day in school without messing up."

"I wouldn't offer this to you if I didn't think you were capable," assured Sandman.

Mona slumped back in her chair. She couldn't take over for Sandman. People like her didn't get to do important jobs like that. Ms. Gloomberg always told her she would amount to nothing. The teachers at school said she was a lost cause. She couldn't agree to become an apprentice, not after Sandman and Torpid had been so kind to her. She would only disappoint them.

"I don't know," she told him. "I need to sleep on it."

"Of course. This decision is not one to be made lightly. By all means, take all the time you require."

"Thank you," said Mona, shifting in her seat and avoiding his gaze.

Sandman stood from the table. "In the meantime, would you like to return to Ms. Gloomberg's?"

Mona's eyes widened.

"You're perfectly welcome to say here," he offered quickly. "Torpid will have finished with your room by now."

Mona agreed. While she may not be able to be Sandman's apprentice, she wasn't ready to return to reality just yet.

4

WHAT LURKS BEHIND THE DOOR

he bedrooms were a deck below the kitchen, positioned at the aft of the vessel just like the captain's quarters on the pirate ships Mona loved reading about.

"Ms. Gloomberg will have a fit in a few hours when she discovers my bed is empty," worried Mona. It was not going to be pretty when she returned. Ms. Gloomberg would skip sending her to the new foster family altogether and ship her off to another orphanage somewhere far, far away, like the Bermuda Triangle, or the North Pole.

"Do not worry about that," said Sandman as he led her through the hallway. "If you decide to return, I shall simply ensure that your home director believes she dreamt you ran away again. It will make a difference from her usual dreams. She has a thing for Highlanders in kilts with knobby knees."

Mona sniggered despite herself. At least that was one worry off her back.

They passed another set of stairs, these leading down to the bottom deck. Mona caught a glimpse of Torpid entering a room at the bottom of the steps with a plate of food.

Mona stopped. She wasn't certain, but she could have sworn she saw someone else standing inside. She doubled back and looked down the stairs but the room door was closed.

Mona frowned and caught back up with Sandman who hadn't seemed to notice her absence. They reached her bedroom for the night and he opened the door for her. "Please feel free to wander and explore the Sanctuary if you wish. Get to know the place and make yourself at home. If you need anything, my chambers are to the left of the corridor, and Torpid's is located to your right."

"What's down in the lowest deck?" she asked.

"Ah," said Sandman, "which brings me to the rules I have on board the Sanctuary."

Mona groaned. "There are rules?" She knew it was too good to be true.

Sandman smiled. "Only two. First, the lower deck is out of bounds. Under no circumstances are you to go down there, no matter what the case, or what you might hear. I trust that you will obey my wishes?"

Mona shrugged. "Sure. What's the second rule?"

"At breakfast, we eat cake," said Sandman.

"I think I can get on board with that," said Mona. Maybe rules weren't so bad after all.

She stepped into her room and had to pinch herself again to make sure she wasn't dreaming. The room was three times the size of the one she and Ally shared back at the orphanage. A huge bed lay on one side with plump pillows and a complete matching purple bedspread. The adjacent wall was lined floor to ceiling with shelves stuffed to the gunwales with books. Mona ran a hand over them, scanning the titles, her hands itching to pick one up and dive in.

The window across the room looked out into the night, and a large brass telescope sat beside it. Next to the window, an open wardrobe revealed an entire rack of clothes, all of which were in her size. Mona shook her head, a thrill dancing over her. It was like Christmas Day, the kind she'd seen normal kids have on TV.

But the best part of the room was the ceiling. It was painted a deep blue and speckled over every inch of it were stars. Ally's stars were cute, but this was something else, like a painter had spent days and days making it absolutely perfect. If she stayed there, she could stare up at them every night until she fell asleep. It was everything she'd ever wanted in a bedroom, like someone had plucked it from her dreams and made it a reality.

"All of this is for me?" she asked, taking it all in.

Sandman nodded. "Good night, Mona. May your dreams be filled with joy and wonder."

"Night," said Mona. "Don't let the bedbugs bite."

Sandman shivered at her words but waved farewell as he closed the door behind him.

Mona dumped her bag in the corner, leaving it packed. She shrugged off her jacket and hung it up in the wardrobe next to the line of brand-new clothes. Mona couldn't remember the last time she had clothes that weren't secondhand.

Maybe, just maybe, Mona could become Sandman's apprentice. This could be a fresh start for her, a new life where she didn't mess up and disappoint people. A life where she could be somebody someday.

A deep yawn escaped her lips and she stretched her tired muscles, reaching for the stars above her. Her eyelids were heavy, but she was far too wired to sleep. She half expected to wake up in the orphanage any minute now anyway, sad to learn it was all some weird dream.

Mona wandered over to what could be her very own personal library if she stayed, spoiled for choice.

Selecting a leather-bound copy of *Treasure Island*, Mona fell back onto the bed, kicked off her shoes, and began to read.

Ten pages later, she closed the book with a snap. Not even an old favorite could distract her wandering thoughts.

The lower deck played on her mind. What was down there? Whatever it was, Sandman didn't want her to know, that was for sure. But why? What was he hiding? She could have sworn she saw someone. Why else would Torpid be taking food down there? It wasn't a midnight snack for himself. His bedroom was on this floor; Sandman said so.

It niggled at her like an itch she couldn't reach. Cake aside, why was keeping out of the lower deck the Sandman's only rule? Why was that, above all else, important to him? If Mona was even going to consider taking Sandman up on his offer, she needed to know the truth—all of it.

Mona tapped her fingers on the book.

Her curiosity was only natural. And wasn't being curious a good attribute to have as an apprentice? Wanting to learn and know all she could? Besides, no one made rules unless they expected them to be broken. Sandman didn't even need to find out. She could peek downstairs, see what was down there, and come straight back to her bedroom. Simple.

A dark thought swept through her mind. What if Sandman wasn't telling her everything? What if all was not as it seemed? It was all too good to be true. Good things didn't happen to her. Sandman's reasons for bringing her here could be for something other than becoming his apprentice.

A cold shiver ran through her, like being touched by a bitter frost. Mona eyed George's bat protruding from her bag.

Mona gave herself a shake. She was being ridiculous. Or was she?

With a deep sigh, Mona put her shoes back on. There was only one way to find out.

Pressing her ear against the door, Mona listened for any signs of movement outside. Certain no one was there, she opened the door just a sliver and peeked out.

The coast was clear.

After a minute or two, Mona slinked out of the room and closed the door quietly behind her. The door never screeched on rusted hinges and the floors didn't creak as she snuck down the hall. Compared to her late-night trips breaking into the orphanage kitchen, this would be a piece of cake.

Reaching the stairs, Mona descended the steps one by one. Bats flapped around in her stomach the farther she went, her palms sweating. She stopped halfway and glanced back upstairs.

Mona squared her shoulders and carried on down the remaining steps. She hesitated by the door.

With a deep breath, Mona grabbed the handle, swung the door open, and gasped.

Afraid Sandman or Torpid heard her, she shut the door behind her and stared around with a gaping mouth. She was right. It really was all too good to be true. The shred of hope tonight had raised within her shattered like glass and crashed to the ground with her punctured heart.

She was not alone in the room.

Someone stood in the back of a barred cell, hidden within the shadows cast by the dim light above. Now Mona understood why Sandman was adamant she not venture down here. It was a prison, and he was holding someone captive.

Mona should have known. Good things never happened to her, so why was she so fast to believe they would now?

Instinct yelled at her to run, to get as far away from there as possible. But where could she go? She was on a flying ship thousands of feet in the air.

The cell lay in the middle of the small room, which had a low, claustrophobic ceiling compared to the other decks and an abandoned feel about it, like no one visited much. Dust coated a table opposite the cell, smudged with activity at the edges where a chair had been pulled out.

Doorways lay at either side of the room, leading off to who knows where. The one on the right caught Mona's attention for a moment, standing out from the other. Where the other was wooden, this one appeared to be made of heavy duty, reinforced steel and had two separate locks along with a thick sliding bolt. Whatever lay beyond, Sandman most definitely didn't want anyone getting into it.

"You're new," said a voice. It echoed around the small room as a figure stepped out from the murky darkness of the prison and stood before her, close enough to the bars that she could see its face.

Mona took a step back, even though the bars separated them. She cleared her throat and asked, "Who are you?"

"Kit. You?"

"Mona," she replied, hugging herself. Noticing this, she forced her arms down and studied the prisoner. Kit had short dark hair and bangs that swooped over one eye with a single streak of bright red down it, like the back of a black widow spider. White skin stood out against black pants and a collared shirt; a slash of red fell from around their neck in the form of a thin tie, matching the scuffed Dr. Martens they wore.

"Are you a boy or a girl?" asked Mona.

Kit shrugged and leaned against the metal bars. "Neither. Both. It's all very fluid."

"Oh, I've heard of that. What's the word…," said Mona.

"I'm genderqueer," said Kit.

Mona clicked her fingers. "That's right. We had an assembly about how some kids aren't boys or girls, and some are both depending on the day. Do I call you he, she, or something else?" she asked, remembering that her teacher said it was important to get it right.

"They, actually. I keep it neutral," said Kit, face mapped in either surprise or confusion.

"They. Got it," said Mona. "So … why are you in there?"

Kit was around her age, maybe a year older. They eyed Mona with intelligent, if not calculating, eyes. "Why? Afraid he'll throw you in here too?"

"Who?" asked Mona, needing to hear it from Kit's mouth before she let go of the final thread of hope that this was all a big misunderstanding.

"The Sandman."

And just like that, the thread snapped.

Mona moved closer to the cell, keeping her voice low. "Why would he lock you up?"

"I'm sure he has his reasons," replied Kit.

"Which are?" she pressed.

"Reasons I don't agree with."

45

Mona watched Kit and narrowed her eyes. "Spit it out. Why has Sandman put you in there?"

"I'd tell you, but …"

"But you don't know," finished Mona.

Kit crossed their arms, shirt sleeves rolled up to the elbows. "Oh, I know. I just don't feel like telling you."

"You know, for someone locked up, you think you might be a bit more helpful to the person who's going to let you out." Mona kept her voice steady, but inside she was verging on panic.

Mona had no idea how she was going to get off the ship, but Kit might know a way. Even if they didn't, two heads were better than one. She needed a plan, fast. She couldn't stay there. For all she knew, she could become Kit's new cell mate if she did. Mona wasn't going to stick around to let that happen and despite Kit's attitude, she wasn't about to leave them. Not when it could have been her in there instead.

Kit nodded toward the door to Mona's left. "He keeps the keys in that room, hanging on the wall. I saw them when that dumb sloth was rummaging around in there."

"His name's Torpid," said Mona, already walking to the door. "And he isn't dumb."

Mona didn't know why she was sticking up for Torpid, not when he was in on all of it with Sandman. Whatever "it" was. The excited creature had been sweet to her before. A bit neurotic, sure, but sweet nonetheless. It was hard for her to imagine Torpid going along with Sandman if his reasons for keeping Kit locked up were for something dark and twisted.

Mona opened the door to find a storage room, filled with knickknacks and extra sailing gear, such as rope and replacement sails, folded into boxes. She took a moment to breathe, out of Kit's sight. Now was a time to think, not panic. Panicking wouldn't get her anywhere, except perhaps a place in the cell.

The keys were right where Kit said they'd be, a bunch of them collected in a round ring. Mona took them, composed herself, and returned to the prison.

The keys jingled in her hand as she chewed on her lip. If Sandman and Torpid were evil, they'd truly played Mona. But then, if they weren't bad guys, why did they have a prison on board the ship? What reason would they have for locking up Kit?

Mona wavered at the cell door.

"What?" asked Kit, hands clutched around the bars.

Mona straightened her back to appear taller and spun the keys around her finger. "I don't know if feel like letting you out."

"Suit yourself," said Kit, though Mona caught a hint of anger behind their eyes before they covered it up. Kit walked over to their narrow spring bed in the corner of the cell and slumped down on it, whistling like they didn't have a care in the world.

Mona saw right through it. It wasn't exactly new behavior to someone raised in an orphanage. People like George acted the same way. So did she when she arrived at a new foster family. Kit was trying to act like they were so unbothered and nonchalant, but it was nothing but a mask to hide behind.

Mona headed for the stairs leading to the upper deck. "Okay, well, I guess I'll be going then."

Kit sat up and got to their feet. "Wait."

"Yes?" inquired Mona, sweet as sugar.

"Let me out." Kit's eyes darted to the side of the room where the steel door stood ominous before flicking back to her.

"What's behind that door?" asked Mona. She went over and examined it closer, running a hand over the cool steel.

"I don't know."

Mona pulled back the big bolt with a screech. "Liar."

"It's nothing," said Kit, their voice raising an octave. "Let me out."

Mona made a show of looking through the set of keys for the right ones. "Something in there you don't want me to see?"

Kit's knuckles turned bone white around the bars. "No."

"I'll take that as a yes," said Mona as she found the right key for the first lock, slid it inside the lock of the steel door, and turned it until a click sounded around the room.

Kit shoved themselves away from the bars and waved an arm. "Fine, go right ahead."

Mona rolled her eyes. "Reverse psychology?"

"You're not as smart as you seem to think," said Kit, like it was a warning.

Mona neared the cage and looked Kit up and down. "I'm not the one locked in a cage."

She returned her attention to the keys and found the final one.

"Stop!" cried Kit.

Mona ignored them and turned the key in the lock. A great hiss released from around the sealed edges of the door, and it opened wide of its own accord.

Jumping back, Mona tried to get a glimpse of what lay beyond, but it was too dark.

A noise came from beyond, a deep growl that didn't sound altogether human. A heavy footstep followed, then another. A silhouette formed around the door frame, wide shoulders almost touching the sides. It stepped out from the darkness and revealed itself.

The air in the room changed at the man's presence. It crackled with energy and fear.

Mona laid eyes on him and knew she'd made a terrible mistake. She felt it deep in her bones. She should never have unlocked the door.

Sandman locked him away in there for a reason, and Mona was under no illusion as to why. This man was dark. Evil.

Long hair, black as night, was tied back from his sharp-featured face. His eyes were onyx, completely blacked out like twin pools of vast nothingness. He appeared ageless, his gray skin free from wrinkles, but he was far from young. Something about his demeanor gave away his many years of life, the same way Sandman did, only where Sandman radiated warmth and wisdom, this man exuded cold hatred.

The hairs stood on end at the back of Mona's neck, every nerve in her body wincing at his presence. His silence screamed danger.

Kit shook the bars of the cell door. "Hey, B. Get me out of here." Kit's words trembled, despite the fake smile they tried to plaster on.

The man snapped his head toward Kit. "You are of no use to me," he dismissed before turning his attention to Mona. His voice was deep and laced with venom.

"Who ... who," Mona stuttered, moving back with each step he took toward her.

Every part of him radiated a great, terrible power. It lay just beneath the surface, palpable in the charged air. He wore a sleeveless tunic and silk slacks, his feet bare on the deck floor. Long, black nails clawed from his fingers, his gray arms veined and muscular.

Mona froze with fear and stared up at him. He leaned down to her height and tilted his head. A wicked grin spread across his face. "Thanks, kid. Sweet dreams."

Before Mona could react, the man threw out his open palm and blew something black into her face.

Bits of grit hit her eyes as a hollow, maniacal laugh bellowed from his lips and echoed in her mind. Mona clamped her eyes shut and rubbed at them with frantic fingers.

Her body weighed a ton and it became too much to stand on her feet.

Mona fell as her eyes rolled to the back of her head. She tried to cling to reality, but it crumbled away into nothingness.

5

DARKNESS

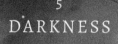

*M**ona opened her eyes to darkness.*

Shadows circled her, whispering and taunting as they passed. Wind howled in her ears, blocking out everything around her. Mona covered her head with her arms, pleading for them to stop, but they only intensified. They grew louder and louder until something boomed.

The shadows burst apart with screeching cries and dissipated into the air. Mona raised her head as they fizzled out to nothing, revealing a place Mona had never been before.

Goose bumps coated her arms.

Mona clamped a hand over her mouth to stop from screaming. The man from behind the door was just a few feet in front of her. His back was to her as he looked out to a massive crowd.

They weren't human.

Grotesque creatures gazed up at the man from below the steps of a large podium. Granite pillars circled around him, holding up a domed roof decorated with sinister gargoyles carved into the stone.

Huge piles of black sand lay all around the podium like a desert made of night.

The grit of the sand rubbed against her bare skin, irritating it. Her head swam, feeling as if she had washed up on a beach made of darkness. Mona stumbled to her feet and took in the crowd.

They waited for the man to speak, watching him with their many eyes. From blood red to slime green, each member of the throng was uglier than the one next to it. From where Mona stood, the monstrous creatures looked like different types of bugs, only gigantic, head and shoulders taller than the speaker before them. Pincers snapped in claps of approval as the man spoke.

"I have returned," he called, his voice reverberating through the mass of bugs.

A rip-roaring cheer followed in guttural grunts and yelps of excitement. Blue flames from torches danced atop the crowd's heads as bugs raised them high in celebration, the light glinting off rows of razor-sharp teeth, horns, and claws.

"The old man couldn't keep me trapped for long. He's weak. Powerless."

More cheering erupted. Mona scanned each side of the podium for an escape, but she was surrounded by the horde of devoted bugs, each of them clamoring and pushing to get as close as possible, though none dared move beyond the steps.

Unable to get away, Mona shifted her weight from foot to foot, rubbing her arms.

The man paced at the front of the podium, reveling in the electricity from his subjects. "The time has come, my friends. We shall rain down on our enemy like a plague of locusts and destroy Sandman, once and for all."

The army roared in response with pumped fists and vicious sneers, louder than ever. They stamped their feet and the entire podium shook from the impact.

Mona backed away toward one of the pillars and, for the first time, the man seemed to sense her. Mona turned to run, but in a flash of black, the man vanished from his place at the podium and materialized right in front of her.

Mona clawed at him, but he grabbed her by the

shirt and pulled her to him. His black eyes bore through her soul.

"Boo!"

6
A NEW DAY

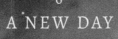

*M*ona screamed.

Someone screamed next to her.

Mona sat up, eyes wide and darting around. She was ready to flee, punch someone, or both.

Her heart rattled against her heaving chest as she took in her surroundings. She was in her bedroom on board the Sanctuary. It didn't make sense.

Torpid's head popped up from the bottom of her bed.

Mona screamed again. Torpid joined her.

"What's going on?" asked Mona, throwing the sheets off, expecting the man with the black eyes to lunge out at her from a dark corner.

"I don't know," said Torpid, scampering to his feet

and looking every bit as confused as Mona felt. "You screamed. And you scared me, so I joined you."

Light spilled in from the window, illuminating the bedroom in warm radiance. There wasn't a bug in sight, and not a grain of black sand anywhere.

"I don't understand," she said, holding a hand over her frenzied heart.

Torpid scooted over and placed a gentle hand on her arm. "Everything's fine, Mona."

"It is?" It sure didn't seem fine a minute ago when the man surrounded by hideous, monster-sized bugs grabbed her. "Nothing is, uh, out of place or missing?"

"Of course not. Everything is where it's supposed to be," said Torpid, brightening to his usual state of giddiness. "I came to wake you for breakfast. I'm making pancakes."

"But," began Mona, still rather dazed. Torpid's bouncing didn't help.

"I'll give you time to get ready. See you in the kitchen," he said and left the room. The door swung back open a second later. "Oh, what syrup would you like? Maple? Blueberry? Who am I kidding? Of course you want both. Coming right up."

Torpid left again. Mona ran a hand through her hair and fell back into her pillow. It was just a bad dream. A nightmare.

She grabbed the sheets and pulled them over her face, taking a deep, shaky breath. She was safe. Everything was cool. It had just been a bad dream.

A laugh bubbled in her throat, and she let it out as relief washed over her. She'd been so worried about everything being too good, too perfect, she'd managed to concoct some horrendous dream about the absolute worst way to mess it all up. Typical.

She had to give her mind props, though. That was some weird and inventive stuff.

It was also one effective way to wake up bright and alert in the morning. Usually it took Ms. Gloomberg a good half hour of insistent yelling to rouse her into semiconsciousness. Mornings weren't her thing.

Shaking her head and still laughing, Mona got out of bed. She stretched and rolled her neck a few times, allowing her body to stop freaking out as it caught up with the situation.

A white robe hung on a door Mona missed the night before. The robe was fuzzy and warm from the heat of the shining sun. She rubbed the fabric against her cheek. Turning the door handle, Mona walked into the best thing she had ever seen.

Her own bathroom. She squealed and danced on the tiled floor.

This was heaven on earth for a girl who had to

share a bathroom with an entire home of other kids. It was a battle each morning just to get up on time to not end up at the back of the line. Given her disdain for early wake-up calls, the water was always freezing by the time Mona got in the shower.

Making the most of this new luxury, Mona took a long, hot shower to wash away the panic and relax her tense muscles. Once she was clean and dry, she padded over to the wardrobe and spent a considerable amount of time selecting a new outfit from the vast array of options inside.

Eventually, Mona decided on an orange T-shirt, jeans, and a purple hoodie the same shade as the Sandman's pajamas. A pair of purple Chucks sat at the bottom of the wardrobe and she shimmied her feet into them. Everything fit perfectly.

Mona returned to the bathroom and sat down at a vanity table with a mirror resting on top. Parting her Afro-textured hair down the middle of her head with a comb, she tied each side into a round puff with some bands and smoothed her edges with a little gel.

The morning had definitely taken a turn for the better. Compared to her horrible dream, it was like night and day.

Refreshed and feeling good in her new clothes, Mona skipped down the hall and headed to the kitchen. She stopped when she reached the staircase to the lower deck.

"It was just a dream," she said out loud in a firm voice. The trepidation rising within her was nonsense, and she tried to force it down. But, if it had been a dream, then what was really down there? And why didn't Sandman want her to know?

Clenching her jaw, Mona brushed away her unease and followed the scent of fresh pancakes. Sandman must have a good reason for keeping the lower deck out of bounds, and she was just going to have to accept it. Simple as that.

For a flying ship with a talking sloth and a man who flew around delivering dreams, the kitchen was a rather mundane sight. Sandman sat at the table with a cup of steaming coffee, reading a newspaper with a pair of wire-rimmed glasses perched on the end of his long nose.

Torpid spotted her from his place by the stove and was by her side a moment later, ushering her to the table and pulling a seat out for her.

"Isn't it a beautiful morning?" he said, waving outside the big window. "The sun is out. There isn't a cloud in the sky. And we have a whole, wonderful day in front of us."

Clearly Torpid was a morning person. Or perhaps he was like that all the time. Mona sat down and awaited her pancakes. She was going to need to eat a lot of them if she was to match the sloth's energy by even a fraction.

Sandman put down the newspaper and tucked his glasses into the pocket of his pajama shirt. "Good morning, Mona. I trust you slept well?"

"Uh, yeah," she lied, vowing to forget all about her troubled dreams. Today was a new day.

"Here's your breakfast," said Torpid, placing a huge stack of buttery pancakes on the table and sitting down next Mona.

Mona's mouth watered in anticipation as she eyed the fluffy goodness. She grabbed a fork and dove in.

"Wait, I thought you guys ate cake for breakfast?" she asked as she chewed. "Though I guess pancakes technically are a type of cake."

Torpid slid another plate under her nose just as she stopped talking and clapped his hands. Four cupcakes lay before her, spelling out her name with a letter adorned on each one. "I made these especially for you. Taste them. They're red velvet with cream cheese frosting."

Not needing to be told twice, Mona scooped up the first one and took a bite.

Torpid wrung his hands as he watched her eat. "Do you like it? Yes? No? Oh dear. You don't. They're terrible, aren't they?" He hung his head and reached for the plate.

"No," said Mona, yanking the cupcakes back from him. "They're delicious."

Torpid wiped his brow. "Phew."

"Thank you, Torpid. No one's ever made me cupcakes before." She held the plate out to him and he took the letter O in his clawed hands.

"Anything for the new apprentice," he said, his big eyes hopeful.

"Have you made a decision yet?" asked Sandman, taking the letter N when she offered.

The terrible, sinking feeling she experienced in her dream when she thought she'd messed everything up churned in her gut like a phantom memory. Mona took another bite of her breakfast, chewing it nice and slow as her thoughts raced.

This was what she had wanted for so long, and now it was finally happening. She had a chance of escaping her preset future as an unwanted orphan trapped in the system. As scared as she was of messing up for real, she couldn't refuse Sandman's offer and return to Ms. Gloomberg's. Not now. Not when a ticket out was sitting right there for the taking.

Somehow she would make this work. She would try her best and do everything in her power not to screw up or disappoint Sandman. She had to try; she had to do this for herself. Besides, there was no way anything she did could be worse than what had happened in her nightmare.

Mona put down her fork and met Sandman's eyes.

"I'll do it," she said. "I'll be your apprentice."

7

FEAR UNLEASHED

orpid jumped up at Mona's words and wrapped his furry arms around her in a hug so tight, it squeezed the air from her lungs.

"I'm so glad you're staying with us, Mona. We're gonna be good friends. I can tell."

"Thanks," said Mona, returning the hug with an awkward pat on the sloth's back and wriggling free from his embrace.

Sandman smiled at her from across the table, his white teeth gleaming. "Excellent," he said with a clap of his hands. "I am thrilled you wish to learn the art of Dream Weaving. We have a lot of work to do."

"I'm ready to do my best," said Mona as she wiped her sweating palms on her new jeans. Nerves crept into her mind like menacing demons now that she had made her choice. They planted seeds of doubt and left them to bloom under the rays of her blinding insecurities.

"That's all I ask," said Sandman, getting up from his chair. "Though I believe you will display quite the talent for sand work. You can already hear it."

"Can't everyone?" asked Mona, getting up from her seat too.

"Yes, after time and practice. It takes a particularly strong-willed and creative mind to be able to hear it untrained. I have big hopes for you."

Mona rubbed the back of her neck. "No pressure, then."

"You have nothing to worry about," he assured.

"Yeah," said Torpid, already clearing away breakfast. "You'll be great."

"When do I start, you know, apprenticing?" she asked Sandman.

"Today, if you wish."

"Really?"

"Of course. Time is precious and we best not squander it." Sandman motioned for her to follow him. Mona ate one last forkful of her pancakes and took the rest of her cupcake with her. It was too delicious to just leave it there.

They left Torpid in the kitchen and walked through the hallway.

"What about Ms. Gloomberg?" asked Mona, having to take two steps for every one of Sandman's thanks to his brisk pace.

"I will deal with all of that. I'm sure once I speak with her, she will be happy to entrust you to my care."

"At this point, I think she'd be happy to entrust my care to a donkey," said Mona. Getting rid of her would be like Christmas morning for the home director.

"Now," said Sandman in a firm voice, "while you and Ms. Gloomberg may not see eye to eye, she has nevertheless cared for you throughout the years. For that, we must remember to be grateful."

Mona lowered her head as warmth spread to her cheeks. While she may not agree with Sandman on that one, she refrained from biting back. Sandman had an air about him that required respect, like that one teacher at school no one messed with even though they never raised their voice.

They walked in silence for a moment, passing the sand factory with the waterfall and turning the corner to a new spot they had not ventured the night before. An arched doorway sat at the end of the hallway, and Sandman led Mona inside.

"This is where we'll spend most of our time," he said as he brought his hands together and parted them the same way he'd done on the top deck. Like the sails, the curtains around the room parted to let the light from outside fill in.

Two maple desks sat in the center of the room with a plush chair tucked under each one. Beside it, a chalkboard was propped on a stand with the words "Welcome Mona" written on it.

It was a round room, decorated with a white marble floor and sky-blue walls. From what she could tell, it was positioned at the front right corner of the ship from the way the windows wrapped around three-quarters of the curved wall.

Between all the windows, large canvas oil paintings hung in gilded frames, each with a different face watching them. Mona immediately recognized one to be a younger Sandman. He sat wearing pajamas similar to the ones he wore now, his face free from the wrinkles of time, not to mention a beard. His hair was long where it was now cropped short and a light mouse brown instead of silver.

The other faces, Mona had never seen before. "Who are these people?" she asked.

"They were Dream Weavers," answered Sandman, solemn.

A young woman with drapes of red hair posed in the canvas closest to them, a dusting of freckles covering her pale face. Her nightgown flowed out over the floor in emerald green, giving her the look of a princess from a fairy tale.

A black woman with piercing eyes and a mischievous grin sat inside the next canvas wearing an aqua-colored robe, her long hair falling over one shoulder in beautiful beaded braids. Mona ran a hand down the frame, taking in the woman. Maybe she could do this after all.

"Where are they now?"

"Dead."

Mona circled the room, examining each of the portraits. Ten people in total, six women and four men. All of them dead except for the man before her. "What happened to them?"

Sandman gave a sad, heavy sigh. "They died."

Mona frowned at his elusive answer, storing the question for another time. Whatever had happened to the nine faces on the wall, it wasn't death from old age. Sandman was literally centuries old.

A vacant space stood out on the wall across the room, the large rectangular outline of another painting evident from the way the paint on the wall hadn't faded as much as the rest of it. The picture had been moved.

"Sandman, do you mind if I ask some more questions?" she said, mindful not to be too annoying.

Mona's teachers always complained she asked too many questions.

"Of course not," said Sandman, looking a little perplexed. "You have much to learn and I encourage you to ask as many questions as you wish."

Mona did a double take. Sandman wasn't joking. At Ms. Gloomberg's, curiosity looked suspicious, but not here. Sandman seemed interested in what she was thinking about and had to say. Heat spread over her cheeks as Sandman waited for her question.

"You conjure dreams for everyone, right?" Mona continued.

"I do indeed."

"What about nightmares? Do you give them to people too?"

"Oh, no," said Sandman, distaste dripping from his words. "I deal in dreams to help delight and inspire. Nightmares are a nasty business."

"Then how do they happen?"

Opening his mouth to answer, Sandman hesitated and closed it again, his eyes drifting to the vacant space on the wall. Of all the questions Mona could have asked him, this appeared to be one he didn't want to answer.

"That, my dear, is a conversation for another time. Now, why don't you run along and collect the case from the wardrobe in your room. It contains all the things we'll need to begin your first lesson." Sandman took out an old pocket watch from his pajamas and checked the time. "I shall go sort things out at the orphanage and meet you back here on the hour."

"But that's in ten minutes," said Mona. "How can you go to the orphanage, speak with Ms. Gloomberg, and get back here in that time?"

Sandman shook his watch. "Time."

"Ah," said Mona, remembering his comment about Old Father Time.

"I best be on my way," he said before Mona could ask him about Santa Claus, the Tooth Fairy, and everything else she believed to be nothing but stories for little kids.

"Okay," said Mona, storing those questions for later too. "See you soon."

She left the classroom and returned downstairs to her room, averting her eyes from the stairs to the lower deck as she passed.

The suitcase was right where Sandman said it would be, a fancy-looking thing made of purple leather and a golden handle. Mona took it out and placed it on her bed. It clicked open and revealed two items. The first was some kind of belt. All around it were empty pouches closed together with drawstrings. Whatever it was for, it wasn't about to win a fashion award anytime soon. The next item was a glass vial attached to a chain necklace. It was in the shape of a star with a stopper on the top point and empty like the pouches on the belt.

Mona had no idea what these things were for. She'd hoped there would perhaps be a dream catcher or something to help keep away unwanted nightmares. Mona never remembered her dreams until last night, and it was far from swimming with dolphins or winning a baseball game, like Ally and George.

Maybe she could ask Sandman for something to help keep the nightmares away if they continued. If anyone would know how, he would. Then again, he wasn't exactly forthcoming when she brought them up. He'd changed the subject and then left, just like he did last night when she asked about the lower deck.

The spark of an idea ignited in her head. No, she shouldn't. She'd promised she wouldn't. Doing it in her dream was bad enough, and it was probably best not to break any rules on her first day as Sandman's apprentice.

But Sandman was away. She could go look and be back at the classroom before he returned. Whatever lay down there, it couldn't be as bad as her dream. Once she knew what it was, she could focus her full attention on her lessons. After all, she needed to do well if she was going to take over from Sandman one day. Any distractions would only undermine her progress. Time was precious like Sandman said, and she couldn't waste any more of it on what was down there.

Mona placed the belt back into the suitcase and closed it, keeping the star vial in the pocket of her hoodie for luck. Before she could change her mind, she headed straight for the stairs and descended to the belly of the ship.

Mona put the suitcase down at the door and took a deep breath, holding on to the star now. She turned the handle and nudged the door open.

What she saw punched her in the gut like a fist.

The room from her dreams. The cell. The steel door.

Mona gripped the door so hard it hurt, using it to keep her legs from falling under her, her other hand tensing so much it was a wonder the glass vial didn't crack.

A familiar face stepped into the light and watched her through the prison bars. "I hope you've come back to let me out."

"Kit," she whispered.

"Mona."

Her mouth grew dry. "You're, you're real."

Kit raised an eyebrow. "Last time I checked."

The room began to spin, Kit's voice sounding far off. Mona lowered her head, her brain swimming. This wasn't happening.

"But if you're real and it wasn't a dream, then that means …" Mona stole a glance at the steel door.

"Yup," said Kit in a wry, pointed tone.

Blacked-out eyes. Gray skin. Sharp nails.

"Who is he?" she said, wrapping an arm around her waist, her pancakes threatening to come right back up.

Kit sniggered and shook their head. "You have no idea what you've gotten yourself into, do you?"

"Tell me," she ordered. Part of her didn't want to know, wanted to hide under her bed and pretend that everything was okay. But it wasn't.

Far from it.

Kit leaned forward and stared her right in the eyes. "You unleashed the Boogie Man."

Mona's heart plummeted. The vial slipped through her fingers and fell to the floor. It smashed over the deck and shattered into a thousand crystal pieces.

What had she done?

8

DARKNESS DESCENDS

⋯⋯⋯⋯⋯

The Boogie Man.

Mona ran out of the cell room, taking the stairs two at a time, Kit's calls echoing behind her.

It was real. Last night had actually happened.

How could she have been so stupid? It wasn't a dream. It was a living nightmare, and things weren't okay. They could have been, but she messed things up in record time.

The man with the blacked-out eyes—the Boogie Man—was real. He was real, and she had let him out of his prison. No wonder Sandman kept him locked away down there, trapped behind the steel door with multiple locks.

Mona had worried about Sandman's reasons for keeping a prison on board, had questioned his motives when he had been nothing but kind and generous to her. She should have known he was doing it for a good reason. She sensed the evil from Boogie Man the second she laid eyes on him. Sandman was keeping him banished, locked away where he could do no harm, and she had let him out. Unlocked the door and unleashed a monster from the darkness. All because she couldn't follow a simple rule.

Mona didn't know how Kit played into it all, or why she somehow saw Boogie Man in her nightmare that followed his release, but it didn't matter. She had ruined everything.

Sandman wouldn't want her as his apprentice now.

Why couldn't she have just stayed in her room and done as she was asked? Why did she need to stick her nose into things that didn't concern her?

Mona ran into her bedroom and slammed the door shut, leaning against it for support, her shoulders heaving.

Sandman didn't know. He didn't know what she had done.

Yet.

It was only a matter of time before he did. Once it was out of the bag, she'd find herself right back at the orphanage where a furious Ms. Gloomberg would send her away.

This was it. The ultimate screwup.

Mona grabbed her backpack and started packing her things. Her new beginning was gone, obliterated before it had even started.

She stuffed Mr. Gordo and the baseball bat into the bag and went to the wardrobe for the clothes she'd brought with her. She wouldn't take the new clothes. They were for the new apprentice, and she wouldn't be an apprentice for much longer.

How was she going to tell Sandman? She couldn't keep it a secret. He'd find out soon, and she didn't want him to think she was hiding it from him, not after all he had done for her.

The monstrous bugs. The army. The black sand.

Mona rolled her clothes into balls and shoved them in along with her other things and zipped up the backpack. Packing done, Mona paced the room, biting her nails. There was no lying her way out of this. There was no fixing what she'd done. She couldn't apologize and hope Sandman would forgive her. How could he forgive her after she'd unleashed the Boogie Man, for crying out loud? She hadn't meant to do it; she didn't know.

But that didn't matter. Unaware at the time or not, Mona had screwed up on an epic level.

The door knocked. Mona froze.

"Mona," came Sandman's voice.

What was she going to do? She plopped down on

her bed, numb and dumbstruck on what to say, on how she was going to break the news to the man who had given her a chance at a new life. A chance she had squandered all because she'd refused to adhere to one stupid rule.

"Come in," she said with a shake in her voice.

The door opened. "I was waiting in the classroom for you," he said as he entered, then stopped. His brow furrowed at the sight of her sitting there and the full backpack lying at the foot of the bed. "Is everything all right?"

Mona dipped her head and watched her feet, unable to meet his eyes.

"No."

Sandman crossed the room and sat next to her. "It's quite all right. I've sorted everything out with Ms. Gloomberg. You don't have to go back to the orphanage."

"It's not that," she said.

"Have you had second thoughts about becoming my apprentice? You can change your mind, you know. Nothing is set in stone."

"No, I want to be your apprentice. It's just …" Mona peered up and lost her words when she looked at Sandman's kind, old face.

He got up, the weight of the bed shifting as he did, and waved an arm. "Come with me."

Mona followed him with slow, uneasy steps, her mind searching for the best way to break the terrible news.

Not even the sight of the sand factory could cheer her up. Once inside, Sandman stopped at the bags of sand under the dispensary and cleared his throat.

"Sand is a tricky thing to master. The ability to create something as intricate as a dream takes years of study and hard work. You have to know how to combine just the right amounts of each color to make it work, and you have to know the person you're building the dream for so their mind accepts and believes what they are seeing as they sleep."

Mona listened on and a pang of emotion struck her heart at the realization she would never create dreams of her own. Never go through the years of study he spoke of. Once he knew the truth, she wouldn't be his student. She wouldn't be a Dream Weaver like the woman with the braids in the painting.

"The first step for any new apprentice," continued Sandman, "is mastering the individual colors. Before you can concoct dreams, you must be able to bend the sand to your will, to create something entirely from the grains."

He scooped up a handful of red sand. "Objects are the easiest ones to get right. Emotions and memories can get tricky. Not to mention messy."

Sandman stared at the sand and as he did, it began to move and collect, solidifying into a cupcake just like the ones Torpid had made for Mona. A wave of his hand and it was back to sand in an instant.

Returning the sand back to the bag, Sandman dusted his hands and said, "Try it."

Mona hesitated. She shouldn't be doing this. She had no right. Sandman needed to know what she had done, but the words wouldn't come. She should spit it out and face the consequences of her actions, but the truth refused to leave her lips.

She moved closer to the bags.

"Select a color," instructed Sandman.

Mona chose orange and cupped her hands together so she held a nice pile of the glittering sand.

"Now listen. What can you hear?"

Mona leaned her ear to the sand and waited. The strange sensation she'd experienced yesterday returned as the sand twinkled at her in some kind of magical, wordless language. Images of sunshine and laughter danced in her mind as she listened, filling her with a contented feeling of sunbathing on a hot summer's day. "It's happy," she said.

"Okay, now close your eyes and focus. Picture an object in your mind that makes you happy. Imagine the sand gathering and molding itself into reality. Will the sand to do as you ask. Feel it forming into the object in your mind and allow the feeling to travel from your mind to your hands."

Mona closed her eyes and pictured Mr. Gordo. It was stupid, but he always used to make her feel happy, even when things were bad. She pictured him in her mind, his missing eye, and the scar from a tear in one of his ears that she had crudely sewn back together.

"That's it," said Sandman with a spark of excitement.

Mona opened her eyes. Glittering before her and hovering above her hand was a ragged stuffed toy. It was missing legs and one of the arms was wonky, but the ears gave it away as a teddy bear.

"Bravo," said Sandman with a clap. "You see? You can do this. I knew you had it in you."

Mona appraised her creation with chagrin. "But it doesn't look like what I pictured." The warped Mr. Gordo shook above her hand before it fell apart and crumbled into nothing, leaving a pile of sand at her feet.

She'd failed again. Like always. Mona kicked at the sand as water welled in the corner of her eyes, the warm feeling of summer and happiness lost with the sand.

"My dear girl, you did splendid. It took me months to be able to conjure my first object, and even then, it was nothing more than a misshapen blob of clustered sand."

Mona glanced up at him.

"Come," he said, leading her out of the factory and toward the kitchen. "This calls for a celebratory hot chocolate."

Mona sat in silence as Sandman prepared the drinks. She took a sip of the hot liquid, but she barely tasted it. The delicious chocolate was like ash in her mouth.

She felt Sandman's eyes on her. He sat across from her nursing his own drink, patient and waiting for her to talk.

"You shouldn't want me as your apprentice," she blurted.

Sandman almost choked on his hot chocolate at that. He wiped his mouth, a look of surprise etched on his wise features. "Why ever not?"

Mona cupped her mug and fought to keep her emotions at bay before they spilled over. "I don't deserve it. I ruin everything." It was just like what her numerous foster parents and Ms. Gloomberg always told her. She was nothing but trouble and a waste of space. Letting out the Boogie Man proved it.

Sandman considered her for a time before he spoke again. "Do you know why I chose you as my apprentice?"

"You couldn't stand the noise from my dreams," she said. "You felt sorry for me, but I'm not a charity case." She set her jaw and pushed away her mug. She didn't need anyone's pity.

"I know you're not," stated Sandman. "Yes, your dreams called to me, as do those of many others, but that is far from the reason I chose you. I wouldn't choose just anyone to take over my job, and especially not because I felt sorry for them."

"Then why? Why me when you could've asked anyone you wanted?"

Sandman leaned across the table and took her hand in his. "I chose you because you are special."

Mona pulled her hand away and pushed her chair back. "I'm not special," she said, almost shouting now. Her bottom lip shook and she bit down on it hard.

Sandman nodded. "Oh, but you are."

"You're just saying that to make me feel better," replied Mona, her vision blurring. She leaned her head down in her folded arms before the first tear fell.

"I believe in you, Mona."

Time seemed to stop at his words. It took Mona a moment to register what he'd said. She raised her head, too shocked to care if he saw her cry. "You what?"

"I believe in you."

Mona stared at Sandman with her mouth agape.

There was no humor in his words, no malice across his face. He was serious. He meant it.

He believed in her.

No one had ever said those words to her before.

She sat unmoving, unable to talk or do anything as he came to kneel before her. Sandman pulled out something from under the collar of his pajamas, a chain, and took it off from around his neck.

He held the chain in his hand, showing her the pendant attached to it. It was a glass vial, like the empty one she'd found in her briefcase along with the leather belt, the one she'd dropped, which now lay broken down on the lower deck.

Unlike her star, this vial was in the shape of a simple bottle with a stopper. Where hers had been empty, Sandman's vial was filled with radiant golden sand that glowed even in the morning light.

"This vial is my most prized possession," said Sandman, holding it with gentle fingers. "It has importance beyond measure, far more than I can express with mere words."

He reached out and placed the chain over her head to rest around her neck. "I want you to look after it for me."

Mona clasped her hand around the vial, the tinkling far stronger from the small amount there than from all the other colors of sand in the entire factory.

"I trust you to keep it safe," said Sandman, "and even if you don't believe in yourself, know that I do, and that I always will."

And he did. Mona could see it in his blue eyes. He believed in her when nobody else ever had.

Which only made things worse.

Tears fell again from her eyes and she sobbed into her hands.

"Everything is okay," assured Sandman.

Mona shook her head with vigor, the weight of her guilt crushing her so much, she found it hard to breathe. "No, it's not," she cried.

Sandman took her by the shoulders, his face worried. "What do you mean?"

Mona rubbed her eyes and took a deep breath. "I need to tell you something."

But before she could tell him everything, an alarm rang through the Sanctuary.

9

THE BOOGIE MAN

*he siren wailed.

It cried out in an earsplitting howl that shook the entire ship.

Sandman's eyes widened and Mona saw fear envelop his features in a way that sent chills down her spine.

Without a word, he got up from in front of her and to the kitchen door with purpose and haste in his stride.

Sandman stopped by the door and turned to her. "Whatever happens, I want you to stay here and hide."

Mona got up from her seat, wiping her wet face. "But—"

"No, Mona," he said, sharp enough to make her

silent. "Hide and do not come out until I find you, do I make myself clear?"

Before Mona could respond, the kitchen door flew open and the sloth ran inside, shutting it behind him. His eyes were wide with terror.

"B-b-b-b-b-b-b," stuttered Torpid before yelling, "bedbugs!"

The door crashed open, hitting Torpid in the back. He flew across the room and collided with the wall, falling to the ground in a crumpled mess of fur.

Sandman dug into his pockets and aimed sand at the door. It forced itself shut in an instant.

The wood rattled as something on the other side barged into it with guttural grunts. It wouldn't hold for long.

"Torpid!" cried Mona. She ran toward the sloth, but her legs stopped working.

Sandman spun and threw a blast of sand over her before Mona realized what was happening. Her body reeled back and zoomed straight across the kitchen. Mona yelled, but it got lost in her throat, her mouth clamped shut of its own accord.

She tumbled into an open broom closet and the door slammed closed. It hit the frame so hard it cracked open, leaving a slender gap.

Mona thrashed and writhed, but it was no use. She couldn't move. Couldn't speak.

Unable to do anything, she watched from the shadows.

Sandman stepped into view as a massive bug like the ones in her nightmare broke the door. It squeezed through the frame, roaring with drool-dripping fangs. Seeing its target, it lunged in the air.

With a twirl of sand, a sparkling barrier appeared in front of Sandman.

The bug slammed into the barrier with a crunch and ricocheted like a bullet. It flew back and hurtled straight into the big kitchen window. The glass exploded and the bug plummeted out of sight, leaving only its screams behind.

Two more bugs bounded into the room before Sandman could catch a breath. They charged at him with snapping pincers and vicious-looking stingers on their tails.

Sandman dodged the first attack, an open pincer barely missing his face. The other bug aimed for his back, but Sandman saw it coming and pivoted in his slippers, faster than someone his age should be able to. The attack missed and hit the other bug in the face.

The first bug snapped at the second in anger, but they turned their attention back to their target and circled around Sandman.

Sandman watched them like a lion tamer, grains of sand slipping from his fist of magic.

Something caught Mona's eye from the sidelines and her heart leaped. The man with the blacked-out eyes stepped into the kitchen.

The Boogie Man.

Mona tried to warn Sandman, screaming inside as tears slipped down her face.

Seeming to sense the Boogie Man's presence, Sandman removed his eyes from the circling bugs and faced the gray-skinned man.

That was a mistake.

"Hello, Sandy."

"How did you get out?" demanded Sandman. Mona watched on, helpless. This was all her fault.

Boogie Man's hollow, carefree laugh resounded with power around the room. "You didn't think you could keep me locked away for long, did you?"

Whatever Sandman planned to respond with, it was lost when the bugs seized their advantage and grabbed him. Boogie Man raised his arms and black sand flowed from two pouches on his trousers and darted through the air in spears, slamming into Sandman's chest.

Sandman fell limp in the clutches of the bugs.

Mona fought to break free, but still she couldn't move an inch.

Boogie shook his head. "Fool." He snapped his

fingers at the bugs. "Bring him with us. I'm not finished with him yet."

Turning his back on them, Boogie Man tossed more black sand into the air. This time the air ripped open before him, creating a dark chasm from the wound. It expanded and grew into a swirling circle of shadow high and wide enough to fit them all in.

Boogie Man stepped through and his bedbugs followed, pulling Sandman by the arms as his legs dragged behind him.

And just like that, the hole in the air closed, and they were gone.

10

THE RESCUE PARTY

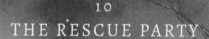

The room was eerie and silent in the aftermath.

Wind whistled in through the smashed window, the siren's wailing gone. The phantom of the noise rang inside Mona's head like a soundtrack to the whirlpool of panic swimming through her.

With Sandman gone, the magic of the sand wore off and released her from its hold. She fell back and crashed into the contents of the closet, brooms and cleaning stuff falling around her.

Mona scrambled to her feet and stumbled out. Glass crunched under her shoes as she took in the kitchen. The table and chairs lay broken on their backs, deep claw marks scratched into the deck's wooden floor in long, permanent scars.

A pile of fur lay in the corner.

"Oh, no. Torpid."

Mona ran over to him and got on her knees. He looked so small lying there among the chaos, his frame unmoving.

"Torpid, are you okay?" Mona turned him over onto his back and raised his head to rest on her lap. "Come on, Torpid, speak to me."

His mouth was open, his tongue lolling to the side. Mona tapped his face. This was all her fault. Poor Torpid.

Poor Sandman.

Torpid roused and a groan escaped his mouth. Then, his big eyes snapped open and he sat straight up shouting, "Bedbugs!"

Mona placed a hand on his chest and hushed him. "Torpid, it's okay. They're gone."

"Oh, good," he said. "Thank goodness Sandman was here to scare them away."

Mona hugged herself. Torpid was knocked out when the door hit him. He never saw what happened after that.

"What?" he asked, taking in her pained expression. "W-w-w-what's wrong?" Torpid blinked and scanned the kitchen, tense and acutely aware of everything, like he was ready to flee at a second's notice.

"They took him," she confessed. "Boogie Man and his bugs took Sandman away."

"What?!" he yelped, leaping to his feet. He paced the room, his fur raised in messier tufts than usual, his nails clinking on the floor. "Oh boy. This is bad. This is really, really bad."

"They walked through some kind of portal," said Mona, dizzy following Torpid's erratic route around the kitchen.

He cringed and ran a hand over the fur on the top of his head. "Oh, no. No, no, no. Not there. This is terrible."

Mona got up and stood in Torpid's way. He bumped into her and made to go around her, muttering to himself, but she grabbed his shoulders. "Where? Where did Boogie take him?"

Torpid gulped and fear projected through his saucer eyes. "The Land of Nightmares," he whispered, quaking under her grip.

"The Land of Nightmares?" repeated Mona.

"It's Boogie Man's home. His evil playground. The whole place is built on fear and horror. Oh, my poor Sandman." Torpid slumped to the floor.

Mona knelt and patted his back.

"How could this have happened?" said Torpid.

Mona's throat tightened.

Torpid shook his head. "I don't understand. How

did he get out? He was locked away. Sandman said he would never get out. He almost died getting Boogie in there and now he's back on the loose."

She'd let him out. The truth was right there on the tip of her tongue. Torpid deserved to know the truth, but if he knew what she had done, that this was all her fault, then he would never speak to her again. He was so kind and welcoming. The idea of seeing the hurt and shock in his eyes, of him hating her was too much for Mona to bear right now. She hated herself enough for what she'd done.

"But can't someone do something?" she asked instead, pushing back the guilt. "What about that Old Father Time guy, or, uh, the Tooth Fairy?"

"Old Father Time doesn't leave his cave," said Torpid, "and getting a hold of the Tooth Fairy is like pulling teeth. Sandman was the only one who could stop him. Now Boogie has him …"

Mona's stomach lurched. "What will he do to him?"

"He wants Sandman's power," said Torpid. "It's what he's always wanted."

"Why?" Boogie Man seemed powerful enough.

Torpid released a heavyhearted sigh. "Sandman makes and delivers people's dreams. They don't just entertain people while they sleep. He plants seeds of hope, seeds that grow and blossom in the minds of every person he reaches. These help people through their darkest times. It makes people believe that things will get better, that they can achieve their dreams and aspirations, and make anything possible."

Torpid sniffed as a pair of big, wet tears slid down to his nose. "Boogie wants to destroy people's dreams. He wants to rid the world of that hope and cover everything in darkness and despair."

What would lead someone to want to fill the world with darkness?

Mona gave herself a shake. It didn't matter. Boogie had Sandman, and it was all her fault. Without him, there would be no one to stop Boogie from making his plans a reality. The world was already dark enough—without hope to carry people along, Mona didn't even want to consider what things would be like then.

"What will happen once Boogie takes Sandman's power?" she asked.

Torpid sobbed. "Sandman's power is a part of him. Without it, he'll die."

Mona's heart skipped a beat at Torpid's words. What had she done? "How long before Boogie takes it from him?" she asked, handing Torpid a tissue.

Torpid blew into it like a trumpet and hiccupped before answering. "Sandman will put up a good fight, but Boogie has ways to make people do what he wants.

It's only a matter of time before it happens and Sandman can't hold on any longer."

It was worse than Mona thought. Her eyes began to well again, but she stopped herself. She didn't deserve to cry over this. She wasn't the one who had been taken away to some nightmarish land. She wasn't the one who would be forced to surrender her power knowing that she'd die in the process and that hope would be ripped from the world. No, she didn't dare wallow in self-pity. Not when all of this was her doing.

"No," she said.

"What?" asked Torpid.

Mona had two options: She could sit there and feel sorry for herself when she had no right to, or she could act. She could do something.

"No," she repeated, a sense of resolve enveloping her the more she thought about it. "I'm not going to let this happen. I refuse."

"But Boogie has Sandman. He ran away to the Land of Nightmares," said Torpid.

"Then we're just going to have to get him back. I'm not going to let Boogie strip Sandman of his powers and end his life. I'm his apprentice, and I'm going to do everything I can to get him back and stop Boogie. Sandman believes in me."

Even if she didn't believe in herself. Even if she didn't believe her own words. Even though she was scared and didn't know what she was doing. Sandman believed in her and she had to try. She had to fix the mess she'd caused and make things right.

"That sounds like a great plan," said Torpid, wringing his hands. "Kinda dangerous, though. Quite dangerous, actually. Okay, extremely dangerous."

"I can't just leave him there," said Mona. "We have to do something."

"We?" spluttered Torpid.

"Yes."

Torpid let out a squeak. "Look at this place," he said, and gestured at the mess. "I really should stay and clean it all. I'll have the place spick, span, and back to the way it was by the time you both get back."

He got up and grabbed a dish towel, fussing over a scuff mark on the floor.

"Torpid," called Mona. "You're coming with me."

Torpid stopped scrubbing. "I am? But …"

"I need you. You know things about this new world, about sand and dreams, that I don't. I am going to need all the help I can get. Besides," she said, rubbing her arm, "I could really use a friend right now."

Torpid tapped his fingers together and looked around.

"I haven't left the Sanctuary for a long time," he said, scratching his neck. "I don't do so well outside.

The world's a scary place, you know?" He stood there for a moment, his mind doing visible overtime.

Then he stopped mumbling, stopped fidgeting, and raised his head. "But I am your friend, and I am Sandman's friend." Torpid squared his shoulders and a look of resolution passed over him. "I'll do it. I'll come with you."

Mona pulled the sloth toward her and embraced him, though she still wasn't a hugger. "Thank you, Torpid."

"Sure," he said with a nervous giggle.

"I just hope Sandman can hold on long enough for us to reach him," said Mona.

"There's just one teeny, weeny, major problem."

"What?" she asked, letting Torpid go.

"I don't know how to get to the Land of Nightmares."

Mona ushered Torpid through the busted kitchen door. "I think I know someone who does."

*M*ona and Torpid journeyed down to the forbidden lower deck.

"Sandman told you about what was down here?" Torpid asked.

Mona mumbled a nonresponse and opened the door before he could ask any more questions.

"Mona. Weird Hairy Guy," said Kit by way of welcome. They were sprawled over their bed, hands resting at the back of their head like they didn't have a single care in the world. "I wish I could say it was nice to see you both."

"Shut up, Kit." Mona had zero patience for their wise cracks. "What do you know about the Land of Nightmares?"

Kit remained quiet.

"Answer me," she demanded.

"You told me to shut up."

"That's it. I'm getting my bat," said Mona, and Torpid had to stop her from leaving the room to go fetch it.

"Well, Weird Hairy Guy," began Kit.

"His name's Torpid," spat Mona.

Kit waved a hand at her and continued. "As I was saying before I was so rudely interrupted, I know the Land of Nightmares. I've been there."

Torpid tapped his foot on the floor with his hands behind his back. "And how would someone get there? I mean, no one in particular. All theory, of course. Say, a girl and her friend, who happens to be a sloth. For example."

Mona rolled her eyes. "How do we get to the Land of Nightmares?"

Kit got up from the bed. "You seriously can't be considering going there."

"I'm not considering it. I am going," Mona told them.

Kit gave Torpid a pointed appraisal and regarded Mona again. "And you think both of you will be able to cut it down there?"

"And why wouldn't we?" snapped Mona, Kit's words too close to her own worries. She had no idea what they were stepping into, or how on earth they were going to get Sandman back from Boogie.

Kit leaned on the bars with a smug grin on their face. "I mean, look at you. You could be a pair of Disney Channel characters. The things down there would eat you up. Literally."

Mona leaned forward and chose her most intimidating face. "You take that back."

Kit bounced back from the bars. "Or what? You're going to punch me? You'd have to let me out to do that. Or come in here."

"What were you doing for Boogie?" Mona asked. She could push people's buttons too. In fact, she was pretty sure Kit had nothing on her in that department. "Why didn't he let you out when he escaped?"

Kit closed their mouth.

Mona smiled. "I don't think he's going to come back for you."

"Black sand," said Kit, their back to Mona.

"Huh?" asked Torpid.

"You need black sand to enter the Land of Nightmares," said Kit. "That's how Boogie opens his portals."

Mona looked at Torpid.

Torpid gulped and nodded. "Sandman has some. He keeps a small pouch of it in the factory for experiments to try to find a way to destroy it. I'll be right back."

Torpid sped out of the room and up the stairs to the deck above.

Mona turned on Kit now that she had them alone. "Did you know what would happen if I opened that door?"

"Yes," said Kit, stepping in front of her, the bars between them.

"Why didn't you tell me?" Not once had they mentioned Boogie Man. If Mona knew what was waiting behind that door, she never would've opened it. None of this would've happened. Sandman would be teaching his first lesson right now, not hauled off to some warped land as Boogie's prisoner.

"I did try to warn you," said Kit. "You chose not to listen."

Mona took a deep breath. Infuriating wasn't even the word. "You didn't try very hard."

Kit shrugged. Mona frowned at them and thought back. Kit did try. They told her not to open the door. Sure, Kit never explained the reason why she shouldn't have, but they did warn her. Why would they do that if they were working for Boogie? Something wasn't adding up with Kit, and she couldn't put her finger on it.

Torpid returned, panting and carrying two stuffed bags in his arms. "I've packed some supplies. Food. Water. Rubber Ducky. Just the essentials." He dropped the supplies on the floor and handed a pouch to Mona. "Here's the sand."

Mona opened it and peered inside.

"There's not much," said Torpid.

"Is it enough?" Mona asked Kit.

Kit reached out their hand. "Let me see."

"Nice try," said Mona. Like she was stupid enough to trust Kit with the sand. For all she knew, Kit would use it to enter the Land of Nightmares themselves and return to Boogie. She opened the pouch and turned it on its side so Kit could see the contents.

Kit considered it. "Enough to get you there. Not enough to bring you back."

Torpid whimpered.

Mona set her jaw, ignoring the pit in her stomach.

"We'll just have to find another way to return. Sandman will know how."

"Assuming you find him, of course," said Kit.

"I will find him," said Mona. She didn't know how, but she would. She had to. "Come on, Torpid, let's go."

"Put this on before we go." Torpid wrapped something around Mona's waist before she had time to protest.

"Nice," sniggered Kit behind them.

"Really? What's with this ugly belt?" Mona asked. It was the one from her suitcase with all the pouches.

"It's to store your sand," explained Torpid. "One pouch for each color. I filled them up for you."

Mona ran a hand over the belt, twinkling coming from each of the pouches at her touch. An odd feeling of comfort arrived with the sand's presence, battling with the uncertainty coursing through her, reinforced by Kit's comments. "But I don't know how to use sand."

"You're Sandman's apprentice," said Torpid. "No Dream Weaver should go to the Land of Nightmares without sand."

"I'm not a Dream Weaver. I haven't been trained."

"It can't hurt. Besides, Sandman said you'd be great. Maybe you can figure out how to use it." Torpid gave her a smile, like it was that simple.

Her attempt at conjuring a Mr. Gordo lookalike was far from good, no matter what Sandman told her. Now she had no teacher to help her master it.

"Whatever," said Mona. She could worry about that later. "We need to get moving."

Kit cleared their throat. "Quick question before you go. How exactly do you plan on finding your way through the Land if you've never been before?"

Mona narrowed her eyes. "Let me guess: you know?"

"Seems to me like a good idea to have a guide," said Kit.

Torpid leaned up and whispered in Mona's ear, unaware he was loud enough for Kit to hear. "I don't think that is a such a good idea. Kit was working for Boogie. That's why we locked them up. They wouldn't tell us what Boogie was planning. We told them we'd let them out once we knew, and they said nothing. We can't trust them."

"Oh, I don't trust them," replied Mona, watching Kit the whole time. "But that doesn't mean they can't be useful to us." She went into the room next door and got the keys to the cell.

"But Mona—"

"No," she cut in. "I don't like it either, but we need them to show us around. Just keep an eye on them at all times."

Torpid looked like he wanted to argue her point, but she glared him into silence. They had already wasted too much time. Sandman needed them.

"So, what do you say?" said Kit. "Do I get to join your weird gang?"

Mona unlocked the cell door. "Fine. But any funny business and I'll make the Boogie Man look like the Easter Bunny."

"Oh, Bunny's quite scary, actually." Torpid shuddered. "With those sharp buck teeth and red eyes."

Mona and Kit stared at Torpid.

"Let's get going," said Mona, before things could get any weirder.

"Just throw the sand and ask it to take you to where you want to go," said Kit with a yawn, as if they weren't about to enter some kind of underworld.

With trepidation, Mona poured the black sand out into her hand. It twinkled at her like the other kinds, but this sand was far from happy. It emitted rage and vengeful wrath, sending tremors of fear through her as she listened.

The sand was heavy in her hand, and shadows wisped around her mind. It was dark, dark stuff.

Mona wasted no time in letting it go, tossing it in the air the same way she saw Boogie do in the kitchen. She closed her eyes and said the name of the Land of Nightmares over and over again.

A zipping sound filled the room and wind whipped at Mona's face. She opened her eyes and saw the portal form in front of them, a pitch-black shadow circling around and around in clawing tendrils.

Torpid was panting and scratching his arms. Mona placed a hand on his shoulder and gave him what she hoped was a reassuring smile. "You can do this," she said. It couldn't be easy for him to leave the Sanctuary after all that time on board.

Kit nudged Mona with their elbow. "If you get scared, don't try to hold my hand."

Mona bumped her shoulder into Kit as she moved toward the portal. "In your dreams."

Mona stepped through the darkness into oblivion, Torpid and Kit right behind her.

11

THE LAND OF NIGHTMARES

*D*arkness enveloped her.

Everything was devoid of light. Mona felt herself being thrashed around, twirling and swirling in all directions with no way of knowing which way was up. Wind banged against her eardrums and blocked all sound but her frantic heartbeat.

She struggled to correct herself into an upright position, but there was nothing but shadow above and below her. All Mona could do was let go and allow herself to spin in a free fall.

A great sucking sound invaded her ears, and the next thing Mona knew, she landed on something with an unceremonious thump.

Something wriggled beneath Mona.

"I think I'm gonna hurl," groaned Kit from under her.

Mona rolled off Kit and met the hard-packed ground. Her head spun, dizziness mixing with nausea in an unfair cocktail as her hand rested on something furry.

Torpid got to his feet and lasted three steps forward before he fell on his face, his eyes spinning around in their sockets.

"I've had better flights," said Kit, their face a pale tinge of green.

"And they didn't even have snacks or an in-flight movie," said Mona with a side-eye. She got up and dusted herself off. None of them appeared to have broken anything on the way, at least.

"What the heck?" she murmured, taking in the surroundings.

Lights from above flickered in and out, giving everything they touched a haunting glow in the looming night. Everything was painted in various shades of washed-out gray or deep black. Mona doubted the place ever saw the sun. Their clothes looked fluorescent compared to the gloom-infested environment.

The lights belonged to a huge sign, hanging above an archway with broken bulbs distorting letters that read WELCOME TO THE LAND OF NIGHTMARES.

The arch stood sentry to a fairground, but it wasn't like any fairground Mona had ever seen. "We have literally entered a nightmare."

A roller coaster was running to their left. The seats were empty, but that didn't stop screams coming from them when the coaster car plummeted down the steep drops.

Directly in front of them, a merry-go-round spun to a creepy nursery rhyme that rang through the thick clouds of mist. Inside, instead of pretty horses and unicorns, gargoyles with tormented faces and headless creatures spun around and around. There wasn't anything merry about it.

To the right lay a water ride. Flimsy-looking lifeboats floated above pools of black, raised high into the air and traveled of their own accord down a slide. It led into what looked like a huge glass fishbowl with rapids crashing inside it. The circling water engulfed the ships from the center, down to the murky depths as gray fins sliced through the surface and swam through the waves.

"Which way?" asked Mona, unable to tear her eyes from the view.

Kit pointed to the fairground. "Straight ahead."

"Of course that's the way," muttered Mona. "Right through the creepy funfair. What could go wrong?"

Mona trudged on, walking by an empty admission booth and through the archway.

Torpid caught up to her and grabbed her arm, holding onto it like he was lost at sea. "Mona, I don't like this."

The rides towered over them. Mona squeezed his hand and faced forward, keeping her eyes from straying to anything else she didn't want to see. "It's okay," she lied, her voice higher than usual.

A screech came from high above.

Torpid yelped, his cry echoing through the empty park like a megaphone.

"It's just a bat or something," Mona assured, glancing up to the starless sky.

"Or something," said Kit, lagging a few steps behind.

"You're not helping," said Mona.

Torpid shook so hard, it rattled her arm. "Maybe we should go back home to the Sanctuary." He tugged her back the way they came.

Mona pulled away. "We can't. There was only enough black sand for one way." Besides, they weren't leaving until they found Sandman.

"There could be another way home. Like a fire exit or something. It's too dark. There's too much open space."

"Keep it down," hissed Kit. "You're both being too

loud."

Mona spun on Kit. "Don't tell me to keep it down. And Torpid, I know it's scary but please, try to calm down. Take some deep breaths."

Mona kneeled close to him and placed a hand on his back. Torpid had been used to four walls for so long. Wandering out into the real world, a nightmare world at that, must have been quite the shock.

Torpid sucked in a lungful of air and blew it out, spluttering as he did, his eyes darting from left to right like he expected something to jump out at them.

"That's it," soothed Mona.

"Sshhh!" repeated Kit.

"You sshhh!"

"We need to be quiet," warned Kit. "There's no telling what's lurking behind the shadows."

Mona stopped dead.

"I'll hazard a guess to say a whole bunch of terrifying clowns with big sinister smiles, razor-sharp teeth, and bulging eyes in colors as bright as their wigs."

Kit raised an eyebrow. "That's oddly specific."

Mona reached out and turned Kit's chin to face an entire circus of horrific clowns.

Kit's eyes bulged. "Oh, right."

Dirt covered the clowns' polka-dot jumpsuits; their round, blood-red noses glinted under the opaque glow of the welcome sign.

"What should we do?" asked Torpid, knees knocking.

One of the clowns, a blue-haired giant with huge feet, broke from the crowd and let out a riotous laugh. His cackles were soon joined by the rest of the clowns in a choir of ill intent and hunger.

"I'm gonna go with RUN!" Mona spun on her heels and booked it in the opposite direction from the clowns, delving deeper into the fairground.

"How do we get out of here?" she called to Kit as they rounded a huge Ferris wheel, spinning so fast the carriages blurred.

"I don't know," panted Kit, leveling with Mona as they pelted down a hill lined with stalls offering squawking creatures as prizes to anyone who could knock down a tower of bottles.

"You're supposed to be our guide!" yelled Torpid, struggling to keep up.

"I lied," said Kit, their long legs propelling them forward. "I've never been here before."

"You what?" Mona stopped and hoisted Torpid onto her back before catching back up with the traitor, her lungs burning as much as her temper. "If we don't make it through this, I'm coming back as a ghost and haunting you."

The trio reached the bottom of the hill and immediately ran out of places to run.

"Oh no!" wailed Torpid.

They were on a deserted pier, the rotted wood covered in slime and moss. Before them lay a huge expanse of water carrying on to the horizon, the water so dark it melded with the sky.

"Should we jump?" asked Kit, saying "we" like they were a team and Kit hadn't lied through their teeth.

"And go where?" asked Torpid, pacing. "The water goes on forever."

"I can't swim," said Mona, edging to the end of the pier and staring down into the depths below. Her palms grew sweaty.

"Then we're trapped," said Kit, crossing their arms at Mona like it was all her fault.

Mona bit back a reply and focused on the more pressing issue of being chased by sadistic clowns.

"They're coming!" cried Torpid.

Kit groaned. "And they're not alone. Here come Boogie's bedbugs."

Clowns and bedbugs. Brilliant. Just brilliant. Five minutes into the Land of Nightmares and the hellhole was already living up to its name.

"Use the sand," said Torpid, hiding behind Mona.

The sand.

Mona dumped her bag of supplies next to

Torpid's, then ran a hand over the leather pouches on her belt. She could do this. Of course she could.

The sand spoke to her through the material, sending pulses of ease through her tense muscles. Not that she was scared. Nothing scared her.

Mona closed her eyes and listened further.

"Hurry up," said Kit.

"Don't rush me," she barked, trying to focus. The sound of footsteps stampeding toward them grew louder and louder with each passing second. Their enemies would be on them in no time.

Mona opened her eyes. It was no use trying to concentrate with the chaos going on around her. She fumbled with the pouches and undid the drawstrings, choosing them at random until she held a decent-sized pile in her fist.

The clowns and bedbugs were halfway down the hill.

Mona closed her eyes again and imagined a picture in her mind, just like Sandman told her to do with Mr. Gordo. Mona reached deep and concocted a humongous monster, full of teeth, with bulging muscles and spikes protruding all over it. It was horrible, far scarier than anything chasing them. The clowns and bedbugs stood no chance against something this horrid. It was a creature befitting the Land of Nightmares, and it would cause terror in anyone who saw it.

Her monster fully realized in her head, Mona opened her eyes and waited.

"Do it," said Torpid.

"Easy now," she said, biding her time. The clowns and bedbugs bounded down the hill and funneled onto the pier, pushing each other forward like rowdy tourists at a sale for free souvenirs. "Just a few more seconds."

Now!

Mona threw the sand into the air and … nothing.

The sand fell to the ground and merged with the slime under their feet.

The clowns and bugs continued to charge at them.

Mona's heart dropped to her stomach. It didn't work. She'd failed, and now they were toast.

"There," said Torpid, pointing toward the opposite end of the pier. "A boat!"

Kit was untying a knot of thick rope from around the back of a boat, untethering it from the pier. Kit tossed in the bags Torpid had packed for them, full of supplies. The sneak was escaping without them, leaving Mona and Torpid to distract the horde of bad guys while Kit slipped away into the lake unnoticed.

"Come on," said Mona, taking Torpid by the hand and sprinting toward Kit.

Something behind her swiped the air and she ducked, just in time to avoid the clutching hand of one of the clowns. It cackled and grabbed at her again, but

Mona pivoted and aimed a punch at the thing's big nose with her free hand.

It was enough to surprise the clown for a moment, and as he brought his hands to his nose, Mona spun and headed for the boat.

Kit was in the small vessel now, kicking away from the pier.

"Oh, no you don't," said Mona, picking up the pace as more and more clowns and bugs joined in the chase.

Kit saw them and waved, motioning for Mona and Torpid to get in as Kit grabbed a set of paddles and stuck them into the dark waters.

"We're going to have to jump," Mona warned her companion. The boat was six feet from the pier now, and Kit showed no sign of slowing down with the rowing.

"I don't think I can make it that far," said Torpid, his short legs doing overtime to stay by her side.

"You have to." They neared the edge and Mona gripped Torpid's hand tight in hers. She wouldn't leave him behind. "On my count: One. Two. Three!"

They jumped.

Torpid screamed.

They left the pier and flew over the water. Kit had stopped rowing and watched the pair coming toward them. Mona and Torpid just made it, inches away from the boat's edge, and collided into Kit, sending all three of them crashing to the floor of the wooden vessel.

The oars shuddered under the weight of the fall. They slid off the side of the boat and tumbled into the water with a plop.

Mona struggled in the tangled mess of arms and legs and broke free. She crawled across the boat floor and popped her head over the edge.

The clowns and bedbugs huddled on the pier, every eye glaring at Mona, Torpid, and Kit as they bobbed away into the heart of the lake. The beasts growled and screeched in an angry mob, but none dove into the water to go after them.

It seemed Mona wasn't the only one who couldn't swim. That, or the clowns didn't want to mess up their makeup. They tossed bits of rock and broken pieces of wood at the threesome, but the boat was too far for the debris to reach them.

"Better luck next time, you jerks!" yelled Mona. She could've stood up to them one-on-one, maybe; a whole gang was far too much.

The bedbugs didn't follow either. They stood on the pier, waving their talons and claws in the air with angry grunts and roars.

Mona, Kit, and Torpid were safe.

For now.

12

DREAM BOAT

ona, Kit, and Torpid sat in silence, the water sloshing against the outsides of the small wooden boat.

There was nothing around them, black as far as the eye could see, from the onyx sky to the dark surface of the lake. They had drifted far away from the pier now, the lights of the fairground and the enraged cries from the bedbugs and clowns lost in the distance.

Torpid leaned against her, his hairy body giving Mona some heat from the cold that lingered with the fog above the water.

Kit leaned their elbows on the side of the boat. "This is great. Just great."

Mona could barely make Kit out in the night. Their silhouette sat as far from her as they could, though it wasn't far enough for Mona's liking, thanks to the size of their meager vessel.

Even still, just the sound of Kit's voice tipped Mona's frustration over the edge. She'd sat festering since their escape, but she couldn't hold it in any longer.

"You betrayed us," she snapped. "You lied." Kit had never been to the Land of Nightmares. They had as much of a clue about where they were headed as Mona and Torpid did. This revelation only made their job of finding Sandman that much harder. There was no telling how much time it would take to reach him, or if they were even going in the right direction. Time was of the essence. They could already be too late.

"You wouldn't have let me out otherwise," muttered Kit.

Mona huffed. "You got that right."

"What was I supposed to do? Let you come here and leave me in a cell on an empty ship with no way to get off?"

Mona would have let them out of the cell. They could have stayed at the Sanctuary, still a prisoner in the sky, but with free rein of the kitchen and bedrooms until their return. Not that she had any intentions of telling Kit that.

"You're a liar. I should've known better than to trust someone working for Boogie."

"You think you know everything, don't you?"

"I know you tried to run off and leave me and Torpid to that horde back there."

"I was not," spat Kit.

"There you go again with the lying. You're a snake." And Mona was a fool. She should never have brought Kit with them, should never have believed them when they said they'd been here before.

Kit leaned forward. "Believe what you want, but I was trying to come up with a Plan B in case your magic trick with the sand didn't work. Which, I'd like to point out, failed miserably. You should both be thanking me, actually. I saved your hides from becoming corn dogs at the fair."

Mona nudged the two bags with her foot. "And you just happened to take the supplies with you."

"All the less for you to carry if you needed to get away from the bad guys," replied Kit, like it was only logical. "Which you did. The bags would have slowed you down. You think you would have made that jump with them on your backs?"

"You think you're so smart," said Mona, "but I see right through you." Even in the dark.

"I know who and what I am. Unlike you, Miss Sandman's Apprentice. Great work at using the sand back there. Maybe you should have stayed in class and learned what you were doing instead of coming here."

"Class was canceled, thanks to your boss. My teacher is trapped down here." Sandman was Boogie's prisoner, and it hurt too much to even think what the evil man could be doing to him as they sat there, floating aimlessly in the middle of nowhere.

"You should be glad he didn't see that pathetic excuse for sand work," said Kit, their words striking Mona where it hurt.

Glad Kit couldn't see her in the dark, Mona paused and then cleared her throat. "I tried my best."

"Well, your best wasn't good enough," said Kit, folding their arms and turning on their seat to face away from Mona, one half of their face hidden in the darkness.

"Why didn't it work?" Mona asked Torpid.

"Well. Um. I don't know," he said with a shrug.

"You've been around Sandman for hundreds of years. You must know something," Mona pressed. "Why didn't my monster come to life?"

Why had she failed when it mattered? Again.

Torpid did a double take. "Monster?"

"Yes. I had this big, gnarly monster in my head who could have pounded those guys and made them wet their pants." If only it had worked. If only she knew what she was doing.

Torpid shook his head. "Oh, no, no, no. You can't conjure monsters. They're evil. They scare people.

Only black sand can do that. Your sand is made of light. You have to conjure good, happy things."

"So, we're supposed to beat these guys with pretty flowers and cute puppies?" Mona sat up and undid the belt from around her waist and tossed it into the center of the boat. For all the good it did her. What was the point in having magic sand if it wasn't going to help them?

"Those are the rules," said Torpid.

Mona grumbled, bringing her knees up to her chest and wrapping her arms around them. "I don't like rules."

"Clearly," drawled Kit with a pointed edge.

Torpid placed a patient hand on Mona's knee. "Next time, focus on something happy. Maybe the sand will work for you, then."

Torpid made it sound so simple, like that was all it took. But how could something happy take on the things down there? Mr. Gordo couldn't exactly scare away those clowns. They'd use his stuffing as cotton candy.

Kit spun in their seat and reached for the belt. "I'll give it a go. I can't possibly be any worse than you."

Kit grabbed the belt and pulled it toward them, but Torpid lunged from his seat and took the other end.

"Do not touch that," he said, yanking his end. "It is for Sandman's apprentice only."

Kit didn't relent. "Let go, Weird Hairy Guy."

Torpid held his head up, pulled with all his might. "No."

Mona put her hand over Torpid's and added her strength to his side. "Give it back."

"Why? So you can mess up again?" Kit tugged and yanked Torpid and Mona a step forward.

Mona nudged Torpid away so she could get a better grip of the belt and fought with Kit in a tug-of-war. "You're in cahoots with Boogie—I wouldn't start pointing fingers at who's messed up."

Torpid covered his ears. "Stop fighting."

"Quiet, Torpid," said Mona, her fingers sore under the strain. "Leave this to me."

She dug her heels into the floor and leaned all her weight back toward her end of the boat. Kit stumbled forward a bit but didn't release their hold. They held on and pulled, the leather burning Mona's palms.

"Let go," she ordered.

"Fine." Kit grinned, then released their end. Mona fell back, and the belt flew into the air.

It spun around and grains of sand slipped free from each of the pouches and landed in a rainbow-colored shower over all three of them, before the belt landed on the floor.

The effects were instant.

Torpid yawned behind Mona and curled up into a

ball, asleep before his head even reached the makeshift pillows of their bags. Kit stretched their arms into the air and plopped down on the seat, chin resting on their arms and legs sprawled out before them.

"No, don't fall asleep," said Mona. "We need to stay awake."

She shook Kit, but they didn't budge, head lolling to the side. Torpid lay snoring like a foghorn.

"Wake up!" she yelled, though it came out muffled through a yawn escaping her lips.

Mona's eyelids were heavy. She fought to stay alert, slapping her own face, but it was no use. Her limbs went limp, her mind shutting down. Her eyes sealed closed and Mona fell into a deep slumber.

13
PAST NIGHTMARES

*B*lack *sand whirled all around her in a tornado of shadow.*

Mona shielded her eyes from the grit, stumbling forward in the storm. A gust of wind whooshed past and dispersed the sand, revealing her location.

She stood in the heart of a desert. Billowing sand dunes piled high, encompassing her in a valley of cracked rock and dead, brittle cacti. Night had fallen in the barren land and an ice-cold chill swept over it, creating waves in the sand.

A galaxy of stars hung high above, bright and brilliant with the clear, unpolluted air. Mona took a step back as a scarab surfaced from the sand and scurried over her foot.

A voice caught in the wind. A dark-skinned woman

in a yellow sari ran down a dune toward Mona. The woman looked over her shoulder, her eyes terrified, and then lost her balance. She tumbled down the dune, landing at the foot of the valley, her breathing labored.

Mona ran to her. "Are you okay?" she asked and offered her hand to help the woman up.

The woman didn't reply. She didn't seem to notice Mona at all. Her appearance was that of a woman in her forties, harsh and beautiful, with dark eyes and a prominent nose above her full lips. But she wasn't forty. The wisdom behind her eyes gave her away; she radiated the same aura Sandman did.

The woman stumbled to her feet and stole a glance at the top of the dune. Mona followed her gaze.

The Boogie Man.

He strolled down the dune with a satisfied grin turning up the corners of his lips. It didn't suit him.

The woman backed away. "Please, don't do this. Let me go."

"You know I can't do that, Raya." Boogie threw sand into the air and it circled around the woman.

Raya reached for a pouch hanging at her waist, but it was empty. The circle of black sand solidified into snakes and tightened around her, binding her arms and legs so she couldn't move.

The snakes hissed and snapped at Raya's face, but

she didn't blink, didn't move. Her eyes bore into Boogie as he approached.

Mona ran behind him and jumped to land on his back, ready to pummel him with her fists. She fell right through Boogie like he was a mirage and landed in the sand. She turned and looked up at him. No, he wasn't a mirage. He was a dream. Everything around her was a dream.

Mona got to her feet and watched, unable to help Raya. Hunger was in Boogie's eyes, but they were not blacked out like they had been when Mona met him. They were brown, with the whites around the iris. Human.

Raya spat on the sand at Boogie's feet. "You're a monster."

Boogie leaned down and brought his lips to her ear. "I know."

With a snap, Boogie yanked off a chain around Raya's neck. His meaty hand clutched a pendant, a spiraled cylinder containing golden sand, just like the one Sandman had given Mona. Boogie clenched his fist and the glass cracked, shattering into tiny shards before he tossed the broken pieces to the ground, the sand twinkling out and melding with the desert.

A single tear ran down Raya's cheek. She stared up to the stars. A second later, her body crumbled and crashed to the ground in thousands of grains of sand. The sand, a radiant gold, decayed into black.

Boogie let out a ferocious laugh that carried with the wind through the entire desert. He waved his muscled arms in a swirling motion above Raya's remains and the black sand moved at his command. The grains floated toward him and collected in his hands. Then, the sand seemed to sink into his skin like ink and shot up his arms with a whoosh of power.

Boogie tilted his head back, exhilarated and high from the power. Mona shivered when he flipped his head forward—she saw darkness sweep over his brown eyes and leave nothing but vacant obsidian in their place. "Ten down," he said. "One to go."

The sand swirled from the ground and caught Mona in another tornado, obliterating the desert scene and replacing it with somewhere new.

Mona spun and fought to keep her balance as she stumbled into a cobblestoned street.

Night had set and street lamps illuminated the lines of cars parked at each end of the road where she stood. Terraced houses ran the whole length of the street, all the windows dark and silent. Rain fell from a murky sky, making the cobblestones slick and glossy under the lights. It didn't soak Mona though; the raindrops passed through her like she was a ghost.

A red phone box sat at the street corner, traffic

signs next to it showing the way to Westminster and Buckingham Palace.

Boogie turned the corner and entered the street. Mona moved between two of the parked cars on instinct, even though he couldn't see her, and watched on.

His pace was casual and he whistled an unfamiliar tune, like a nursery rhyme that seemed out of place coming from someone so evil. He made it halfway down the street and then stopped. "I know you're here."

Mona ducked down further and covered her mouth to stop clouds of breath forming. Could he see her?

Sandman stepped out from between the line of cars across the street. "Boogie," he said, like he happened across an acquaintance during a night stroll. He looked the same as Mona knew him, gray hair and beard, though his face was a mask of deliberate calm.

"Sandy," replied Boogie, matching his light tone, though both their bodies were tense and rigid. "I've been looking for you."

"Yes, I'm aware." Sandman moved into the middle of the road and shrugged off his cloak, folding it neatly and placing it on the hood of a nearby car. "It appears you've found me."

Boogie sneered and joined Sandman on the road,

thirty yards apart in a standoff as the rain hurtled down from the heavens. Static hung in the air, their power and the charge of the sand in each of their hands palpable and electric.

"You've destroyed them all," said Sandman, his voice wavering.

Boogie smiled. "Not all. I still have you, old man."

"I'm going to lock you away for eternity for what you've done." Sandman's words weren't a threat; they were a promise. He stood on the balls of his feet, ready for the inevitable.

"We'll see about that," said Boogie, and he charged forward.

Sandman bounded forward too, each of them conjuring with their sand. They closed the distance between them and collided in an explosion of sand and magic.

14
WHAT LIES BENEATH

Mona sucked in a huge breath and bolted upright.

She heaved in and out as her mind came crashing back to reality, what she saw in her dream, in her nightmare, etched into her mind forever. Of Raya and black sand.

She was in the boat, Torpid and Kit sleeping around her. The sky above had gone from pitch-black to a dull, dark blue that made her companions look ghostly. The sky was the only thing showing the passing of time, as close to daylight now as they were likely to get down here.

They were still surrounded by water, the fog lingering through the night. Mona squinted and thought she could make out something in the distance, land perhaps, but she couldn't be sure. Maybe she was seeing what she wanted to see, unlike that of her haunted dream.

Mona ran a hand through her hair and took deep breaths, willing herself to calm down. It wasn't real. It was just a dream.

Then again, her last nightmare turned out to be real, so there was no telling what was real and what wasn't anymore. Her head throbbed, and she placed a cool hand over it. Awake or asleep, she was trapped in a nightmare she couldn't escape.

"Hey, wake up," she said, nudging Torpid and then Kit.

Torpid swiped at his face and mumbled, "But, Mom, I don't wanna go to school today."

Mona giggled. "Torpid. Kit."

Neither of them moved, Kit's light snores and Torpid's not-so-light snores remaining undisturbed.

Mona shook them again, harder this time. "Come on, you two, get up."

No response. The sand had certainly done its job. Perhaps too well.

"Hello!" Mona yelled as loud as she could, and this time it got a reaction.

Torpid's big eyes opened and he wriggled around the boat floor like a tortoise flipped on its back.

"Whaaaa! What's wrong? Where am I? What's going on?"

"Torpid," said Mona, taking him by the arms until he stopped squirming. "It's fine. You're safe." Relatively, considering they were in a place called the Land of Nightmares, but her words settled him down.

Kit ran a hand through their bedhead hair and stretched. "How long did we sleep?"

"I think it's morning," said Mona. "We could have been out of it for hours." They'd lost so much time—time they couldn't afford to lose.

"Sandman," said Torpid.

"It'll be okay," said Mona, firmer than she meant. "Sandman's strong. He won't have given up yet." She hoped.

In truth, Mona had no idea how long Sandman could hold on. They had no way of knowing if he was still hanging on, but she had to believe. Had to keep hoping there was a chance to save him from this. To make things right.

Mona glared at Kit, but they were ready for her.

"Don't look at me like this is my fault. You're the one who grabbed the sand from me."

"You shouldn't have taken it in the first place," retorted Mona.

"It wasn't yours to take," said Torpid. "The sand is for—"

"'The Sandman's apprentice,'" imitated Kit, rolling their eyes. "Whatever."

"Enough. I'm not spending any more time on this. Don't touch my belt again," Mona warned Kit, looping the belt around her jeans and tightening the drawstrings of each pouch.

Kit muttered something under their breath that Mona couldn't hear, but she didn't care. There was still the matter of getting off the boat to deal with. Kit could wait. They weren't exactly going anywhere while stuck on board.

Torpid stood and gave himself a shake, like a puppy caught in the rain. "Well, at least we had nice dreams to refresh us. I certainly needed one after last night. What did you dream about, Kit?"

"I'm not telling you anything, Weird Hairy Guy," said Kit, paying deliberate attention to their nails.

"Well, I had a wonderful dream," said Torpid. "I was floating on an inflatable ring in a pool at the bottom of a beautiful waterfall. It was very relaxing. I even had a drink in a coconut. You know, the ones that come with a swirly straw and those little umbrellas?" Torpid made a slurping sound. "Delicious."

"It sure beat my dream, that's for sure," said Mona. A beautiful waterfall and some fancy drinks sounded like heaven compared to the hell she'd woken from.

Torpid cocked his head. "Oh?"

"I had a nightmare."

Kit looked up from their nails at that but kept their mouth shut.

"But the sand wasn't black," said Torpid, a crease on his forehead.

Mona considered the sloth's point. It was the second nightmare Mona had had since her first meeting with Boogie, when he blew something in her face and she blacked out, waking up in her bed.

Black sand. It must have been.

She was about to ask Torpid if the effects of black sand lasted longer than the colored stuff but quickly clamped her mouth closed. Her cheeks burned.

"I don't know how it happened," Mona lied, noting the look Kit gave her with a shake of their head. "It was bad."

"What happened?" asked Torpid.

Mona fiddled with the cuff of her hoodie. "I saw a woman. Raya, her name was."

Torpid straightened. "Raya?"

"Yes. Boogie did something to her. I think," Mona stopped, seeing it all over again in her head. "I think he killed her."

Torpid slumped. "He did."

"How do you know?" asked Mona. "You weren't in my dream."

"Mona, you didn't dream something make-believe. That actually happened."

But that meant … "You mean. Raya's …"

"Gone. Yes." Torpid sniffed.

"Who was she?"

"She was a Dream Weaver. The last one Boogie got."

Mona shared a look with Torpid, neither of them voicing what they both were thinking. Raya wasn't the last one. Boogie had Sandman now. If what Mona dreamt was real, then she also saw the night Sandman managed to capture Boogie and lock him up.

Thanks to her, Sandman's triumph had been in vain. Now he was the prisoner.

"The last one?" asked Mona. "You mean, he got to more of the Dream Weavers than Raya?"

Torpid's eyes filled and grew glossy. "He got them all."

Mona thought of all the paintings in the classroom on board the Sanctuary. Each of them dead as Sandman had told her. Destroyed at the hands of Boogie. "Why?"

"Power," said Torpid, distaste in his mouth. He dabbed at his eyes with his fingers. "He's obsessed with it. He used to be a Dream Weaver, before he went dark."

Mona took a sharp inhale of air. A Dream Weaver.

Boogie was once like Sandman. Was like the people in the paintings. Her mind turned to the empty space in the classroom, the vacant spot that had once housed a painting.

"He betrayed his own?" Kit asked, listening in with close attention.

Mona frowned at them. Did Kit think Boogie was above betrayal? Kit was working for Boogie, and yet he left Kit down in the bottom-deck cell. He told Kit he had no use for them anymore and escaped without them. Boogie wasn't the type to feel loyalty to anyone.

"Terrible, isn't it?" Torpid hung his head. "He was always the weakest of the group, the one most affected by the power of the sand. I never liked him."

Mona startled and moved to sit next to Torpid. It had never occurred to her. Torpid wasn't just talking about a group of people who called themselves Dream Weavers; he was talking about his family, about people he knew and loved. Boogie had taken all of them but Sandman away from Torpid. No wonder he didn't leave the Sanctuary.

"He grew consumed by darkness," continued Torpid, "and craved more power than he had. His sand turned as black as his shriveled heart. He was addicted to it. Was willing to do whatever it took to get more. Even if that meant stealing it from his friends."

Visions of Raya crumbling to sand plagued Mona's thoughts.

"They fought Boogie for years, but one by one they fell, until only Sandman stood against him."

Guilt crept up from where Mona had pushed it down. It barged in like an unwelcome guest and took up permanent residence. Her actions had taken away Torpid's one remaining family member. The only person Torpid had left. Now he had no one.

Wrong. Sandman wasn't gone yet. And Torpid had her now too, if he wanted her, that is.

She couldn't keep it in any longer. It bloated inside her and she was ready to burst from the sheer force of it. She hadn't lied, but she might as well have. She couldn't withhold the truth from him any longer. "Torpid, I need to tell you something."

"What?"

Mona stared at her feet. "Please don't hate me."

"I could never hate you, Mona," said Torpid, giving her a smile she didn't deserve.

"I—" Mona stopped talking and held her hand out for the others to be silent.

"What?" whispered Kit.

Mona strained her ears. She couldn't quite put her finger on it, but something wasn't right. "It's quiet. Too quiet."

Right then, the water around them began to

quiver. It grew more violent and the boat bobbed from side to side.

Mona gripped onto the sides for balance, Kit doing the same and Torpid wrapping his arms and legs around the wood-paneled seat.

With a spray of water and a great rumbling, something broke through the surface of the lake and rose from the deep aquatic caverns below.

Up and up it went until it towered over them. Great big tentacles emerged.

The sea monster roared.

15
MAYDAY, MAYDAY!

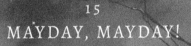

he sea monster's roar hit them in a gust of fetid breath that almost capsized the boat.

The stench of last week's tuna assaulted Mona's senses, clumps of fish guts spattering all over them from between the massive beast's rows and rows of jagged teeth. Someone really needed to floss.

The monster rose to the height of Ms. Gloomberg's three-story home, its single huge eye the size of the second floor alone with its bright green iris homing in on them from above. Its skin was purple, from its hammer-shaped head to the suckers on its tentacles, and completely covered in slime. It dripped off it and into the water in giant drops of goo.

It was part kraken, part alien, and every part terrifying.

"M-m-m-m-Mona," squeaked Torpid. "What are we going to do?"

Mona craned her neck at the monster and her legs turned to jellyfish. Its huge bulk blocked out the light from the dark blue sky, covering the boat in shadow.

"I'll tell you what I'm going to do," said Kit. "Get the heck out of here." Kit stood on the edge of the boat and without a second glance, dove into the water. Their head sprouted through the surface and they began swimming in the opposite direction from Mona, Torpid, and the creature from the nightmare lagoon.

Mona cast a frantic look around.

No oars. No land near enough to reach. No hope.

Ice coursed through her limbs and she stood frozen in the middle of the boat with no way out. She couldn't swim. She was trapped. She had two options, the sea creature or the water, and neither of them would end well.

"Mona," called Torpid, shaking her.

"Huh?" she asked, defrosting a bit.

Just then, one of the tentacles shot out from behind them and wrapped around Torpid. The sloth screamed, and before Mona could react, it swept him off the boat and took him under the water.

"Torpid!"

Mona ran to the edge of the boat and looked down to see bubbles rise from below. A second later, the tentacle rose from the other side of the boat and hoisted a soaking-wet Torpid high into the air.

Torpid heaved and took a great gulp of air, the tentacle squeezing him tight. "The sand!" he called down to her.

Mona placed a hand on her belt. "Sand."

"Yes!" yelled Torpid, as the beast used the tentacle holding the sloth to try to bash Mona from the boat. She ducked, narrowly avoiding a sucker to the face. Torpid's strained voice called out to her. "Use your imagination, and remember, no monsters! It has to be something good."

"Sand," she repeated, snapping out of her fear.

Mona peered up at the creature and ran her hand over the bags of sand. She hadn't come all this way to fall short now. She had a job to do, and nothing, not even a ferocious sea monster, would stop her from reaching Sandman.

The monster rose another of its great tentacles from the water and sent it crashing down, just missing the boat. The impact from the resulting waves battered against the sides of the vessel and it sent the boat spinning across the surface to the right-hand side of the monster, out of its direct line of sight.

Think, think, think.

Something she could use against the beast that was also good. What did people dream about? She never remembered her own dreams. Nightmares, yes, but they weren't helpful right now.

George. He had nice dreams. Sandman had told her so. He dreamt of being a baseball player.

Using the precious few seconds it took the monster to turn itself around and face her, Mona listened to the twinkling of the sand. She chose from the yellow and orange pouches, which called to her most, and held the grains out in her hand.

"You can do it, Mona," cried Torpid as he came into view, trying but failing to wriggle free from the monster's clutches. "Sandman believed in you, and I do too."

They did. They both believed in her and she would not let Torpid or Sandman down.

Mona centered her mind and focused on George's dreams of being a baseball star. She pictured the bat she had taken from him the last night at the orphanage, remembering how the handle felt in her hands, the glossed wood and tape wrapped around it for good grip.

A new weight formed in her hand and she opened her eyes to see what she had conjured.

It was a bat. It wasn't exactly like George's, and it was most definitely crooked, angling off to the left like a tree branch, but it was real and she had made it so.

In her other hand was a baseball, larger than it should have been, but ideal for its purpose.

Mona took aim, squinting one eye and lining up the shot. She'd only have one attempt and it had to be a home run.

Throwing the ball into the air, Mona gripped the bat, pulled it back, and swung with everything she had. The bat met the ball and Mona sent it hurtling toward the monster. It was hard to miss given its immense size. The hit struck true, meeting its target and smacking the creature in the center of its big eye.

"Bull's-eye!" said Mona, pumping her fist.

The sea monster threw its head back, screwing its eye up and bringing its tentacles to cover it from further attack. The instinct reaction freed Torpid, and he fell at full height straight into the water in a belly flop.

Mona leaned over the boat and held her arms out to Torpid as he swam up, spitting out water and wiping slime from his face.

"You did it," he said, and she pulled him on board just as the sea monster let out a furious roar that made the first one seem like a baby's giggle.

Mona gulped. "If by that you mean making it madder than it already was, then I'd say I did it too."

All eight of its giant tentacles rose from the water and

came crashing down toward them. Torpid grabbed Mona and yanked her back, sending them both straight over the other side of the boat and headfirst into the water.

Mona opened her eyes upon meeting the water and saw the great big tentacles ensnare the boat and split it into nothing but tiny, splintered pieces that floated up to the surface above her.

Something grabbed her hood from above and she broke through the surface, coughing and struggling for air.

"Mona," said Torpid next to her, looking like a drowned poodle. "Are you okay?"

Mona's teeth chattered. "I can't." Her head fell back under the crashing waves and Torpid pulled her back up. "I can't swim," she rasped, kicking her legs and trying to stay afloat.

"I've got you," Torpid assured, but just as he said it, the tentacles were back and heading right for them. "Get under!" he said, diving away from the landing spot of one of the beast's appendages.

Mona dove under too and felt the impact of the blow to the empty water. It pulsed through the area in a great wave that sent her spinning away from Torpid in a tangled mess of wet, heavy clothes.

Mona lost sight of Torpid. It was too dark under the water to see far beyond what was right in front of her. She couldn't see him, or the surface.

Mona screamed for him and was met with nothing but bubbles from her throat. She thrashed around, trying to swim without knowing how. Her lungs burned, muscles aching and skin ice cold.

She felt herself sinking toward the unseen depths below. She couldn't think. Couldn't breathe.

Mona opened her mouth to call for help and got a lungful of water.

Her hands brushed a leather pouch and she pried it open with frantic fingers as her mind slowed. She reached out into nothing but darkness, falling deeper and deeper, giving herself over to the water, and thought of Ally …

…

…

…

A burst of blinding light exploded in her blurred vision causing her to wince and clamp her eyes shut. A strange noise carried through the water in a way her screams couldn't. It was followed by two more, similar, but not quite the same.

Something brushed against her and she was too weak to try to get away. It caught her and Mona felt herself rushing through the water. Her head was light, lungs clogged and unable to do their job. Her eyelids fluttered open and Mona saw them.

Dolphins. Just like the ones from Ally's dream.

Three of them, surging upward, glittering amid the water in brilliant bright blue.

They picked up speed and kicked with their tails, leaping through the surface with calls of glee.

Air. Sweet, sweet air. Mona coughed up water and took her first breath.

Her dolphin dove through the air and Mona braced herself to meet the waves again, holding on for dear life. The dolphin submerged but shot straight back up and floated above sea level, Mona secured on its back.

The second and third dolphins were already there with Torpid spluttering on top of one.

"Torpid."

"Mona."

"Let's get out of here," she said, and patted the dolphin's side to tell it to go.

Behind them the sea monster roared and gave chase, but it was no match for the dolphins. They were too fast, swimming expertly through the waves and currents, laughing all the way as the creature grew smaller and smaller in the distance.

They found Kit along the way, sputtering and struggling to cover much distance after fatigue had settled in. The third dolphin scooped Kit up and they lay across the dolphin's back, panting and otherwise silent as the roars from the beast were lost with the waves.

Mona examined her creations as they sped forward in perfect synchrony. The dolphins hadn't properly formed, but given the circumstances, Mona was satisfied. Their skin wasn't gray and white, but a bedazzled blue, making them look like they had rolled around in a vat of glitter. Their shape wasn't quite right either, but Mona didn't care. As long as they took them far, far away from the sea monster.

16

ALL EYES ON US

It wasn't long before Mona spotted land in the distance. The dolphins carried them toward it, and they arrived at a beach in no time.

"Thank you, ladies," said Mona, kneeling close to the dolphins. She stroked each of them on the snout and with a final whistle, they disintegrated back into sand and floated into the water like sea foam.

Mona watched the sand disperse before sloshing up through the shallow water to the stones of the beach where Kit and Torpid stood, teeth chattering against the blistering cold winds. Mona shivered, her clothes dripping and hanging heavy from her frame.

Cliffs surrounded the beach, jagged and impossibly high. Mona scanned the beach for another way through but there was nothing. The climb was too high, the wind too strong, and all three of them too tired after their ordeal.

An opening jutted out from the corner of the beach, at the bottom of the cliff. A cave.

"Come on," said Mona, leading the way. She couldn't feel her toes and her legs were growing numb. They had to get out from the wind's frozen embrace before they became hypothermic.

The others followed without comment, trudging along with dragging feet and sullen faces.

"In there?" said Torpid at the entrance.

Mona nodded. "It's either through the cave or back out to the water with the sea monster."

Kit looked over the water, shrugged, and then stepped inside the mouth of the cave.

Torpid remained rooted to the ground and fidgeted with his fingers. "I don't like this, Mona."

"You can always stay here," said Mona, and then went inside without another word.

Torpid groaned and then, like Mona knew he would, scampered in after her, grabbing the bottom of her hoodie as she navigated over the uneven ground. Mona smiled.

A thud came from in front of her, and Kit swore. "I can't see a thing."

Mona placed her palm against the rough cave wall. "It's too dark in here."

"Give me a sec." Torpid's grip left Mona's and she turned to see him leaving the cave, his silhouette black against the light from the entrance. He returned a few minutes later carrying something that made him appear to have grown a bunch of spindling limbs. The darkness took him as he joined them and the sound of rubbing and scratching echoed off the rock walls.

Sparks danced in front of Mona's eyes and then an orange flame took their place, growing as it consumed the collection of dried grasses and driftwood Torpid had collected.

"Great idea." Mona leaned down to the fire and blew it gently so it would grow. The heat was divine against her cold skin and sodden clothes.

Kit kneeled across from her and held their shivering hands up next to it.

The fire covered everything in a welcome warm glow, the brightest thing to have met Mona's eyes since arriving in the Land of Nightmares. Beyond their makeshift camp, however, the darkness lingered, deeper against the light of the flames that created menacing shadows all around them before completely engulfing the path into the belly of the cave.

Mona averted her eyes from the shadow as a cold shiver ran down her spine. It was just because she was wet, that's all. Definitely not because she was frightened. Of course not.

The fire crackled and snapped, devouring the wood. Torpid ventured out again, seeming all too glad to leave the cave, and returned with more wood to feed the flames. They sat in silence as their clothes, or in Torpid's case, his fur, slowly dried.

"I'll make us something to eat," said the sloth after a while, poking the fire with a stick. "That should cheer us up."

Mona's stomach rumbled in response. She hadn't eaten anything since breakfast back on board the Sanctuary.

Torpid's face dropped. "Oh. The bags."

Mona sighed, her stomach grumbling in frustration. Whatever delicious food Torpid had packed for their travels now lay at the bottom of the lake.

"No s'mores for us, then," said Kit, leaning their chin on their fist like a sullen toddler.

"Now what?" asked Torpid.

Mona peered into the darkness before them, the hairs on the back of her neck on end. "We go on ahead."

"We're going to need a light," muttered Kit.

Torpid bounced to his feet. "Oh. I know. Leave it to me. Be right back." He scampered away again, back out to the beach, and this time returned with three makeshift torches made of twigs bound into a cone shape with seaweed.

"You're quite the handyman," said Mona, taking the torches. The seaweed was slimy and reeked of the ocean, but it would stop the fire from traveling down the torches and burning them.

Mona went to the fire and lit the top of the first torch. She handed it to Torpid with careful hands so as not to accidentally catch his now dry and fluffy fur. Then, she lit her torch and secured the third through a loop in her belt as a spare in case they ran out.

"Don't I get one?" asked Kit.

Mona put her hands on her hips. "Only people I trust get one."

"That's not fair," said Kit. "You can't expect me to go down there without a torch."

"I don't expect you to do anything," replied Mona. Except leave them for dead the next time they ran into trouble. Kit was two for two on that one.

Kit held out their hand. "Give me a torch."

Mona took a step back and thrust the light to shine on Kit's face. "Why are you still here? You could have run off back to Boogie by now." Kit had tried to get away, sure, but not from her and Torpid. Kit had only made a run for it when their own life was in danger.

Kit frowned. "Why would I want to do that?"

"Oh, I don't know, maybe because you work for him."

"No I don't," snapped Kit, their voice traveling

into the shadowed tunnel before them. "Stop saying that!"

"You do," piped up Torpid. "Sandman caught you trying to get on board the Sanctuary."

"Sounds to me like you were caught red-handed," said Mona, glaring at Kit.

Kit sighed. "What it sounds like and what it was are two very different things."

"They never spoke to Sandman," Torpid told Mona. "Kit refused to talk. To betray Boogie. That's why we had to lock them up. Every day Sandman asked them, and every day they refused to speak."

"You don't know what he would have done if I told Sandman anything."

"What do you mean?" asked Mona, eyes narrowed. Kit was as slippery as a fish, and she didn't trust them as far as she could throw one of Boogie's bedbugs.

Kit's shoulders slumped, the flames highlighting the heavy bags under their eyes. "I wasn't working for Boogie by choice. I was doing it because I had to."

"You don't have to do anything," said Mona. "You had a choice."

Just like she had a choice. A choice of whether to go down to the lower deck against Sandman's will or not. No one had made her do that. It was all her fault. What she did was on her, and she wasn't going around blaming everyone else for her own actions. Kit's excuses weren't going to fly with her.

"I did have a choice," replied Kit. "And I chose to keep my family safe."

"Your family?" she said, the idea of Kit having a family not occurring to her until now. Most of the kids she knew didn't have families. A pang of jealousy jabbed at her gut. Why did Kit get to have a family and she didn't?

"Boogie threatened to hurt them if I didn't do what he said." Kit's eyes were glossy in the firelight. Guilt wiped out the jealousy inside Mona.

Torpid covered his mouth. "Oh, that's terrible."

"Sandman could have helped you. You should've told him." Just like she should have told Sandman about letting Boogie out. If Mona had told him sooner, then maybe none of this would have happened. Boogie wouldn't have been able to ambush Sandman unawares.

Kit shook their head and tears slipped from the corner of their eyes. "I couldn't take that risk. Not when my family was involved." Kit's voice shook. "I haven't seen them in months. They must think I've run away and left them, but I will do anything to keep them safe. So lay off me, okay? I did what I had to."

Mona opened her mouth in retort but closed it again. She didn't know what to say, what to feel. She itched at her arm and tried not to meet Kit's tearful eyes.

Torpid walked over to Kit and hugged them, much to the chagrin of Kit. They slid free from the sloth's embrace, but Mona thought Kit let Torpid hold on for just a few seconds longer than they had to.

"A few months?" asked Torpid. "But Sandman caught you the night before he captured Boogie. That was a few weeks ago."

Mona listened on. So that was when Sandman had taken down Boogie. In London, just a few weeks ago. All those years and people lost, Sandman had finally stopped Boogie, only for her to waltz in and mess it up soon after.

"Boogie wanted me to break into the ship," said Kit, answering Torpid. "He spent months planning it out and I was forced to tag along."

"Why you?" asked Mona, snapping out of her thoughts.

"Boogie wanted to get to Sandman and he thought he could do it through me. He was wrong."

"Yeah, but why did Boogie choose you specifically?"

"I get night terrors sometimes," said Kit, staring into the fire, a haunted look crossing their face. "They always seem so real. One night I had a really bad one about a man with blacked-out eyes, only when I woke up, he was there, in my bedroom. Boogie said the nightmares drew him to me, that I'd be the perfect pawn for him."

Sandman had been drawn to Mona because of her dreams. He'd said so the night he came for her. The same thing happened to them both, only Kit drew the short straw on which Dream Weaver turned up to take them away. Had things been different, Boogie could have come for her. She could have been Kit.

Mona didn't know what it was like to have a family. She didn't know what it was like to have their safety threatened and held as ransom to do someone's bidding. If someone did that to Ally, Mona would do anything they wanted. Without question.

"Look, Kit. I—" Mona stopped and tripped over the words.

Kit huffed. "You're apologizing now?"

"Trying to," she said. "I'm sorry for, well, you know." Mona scratched the back of her head and looked at Kit. Apologies weren't her strong suit. Mostly because she was never wrong, or at least never admitted to it when she was.

Kit allowed a small grin to spread from the corner of their mouth. "Me too. I'm sorry for bailing on you guys."

"And I'm sorry for being kinda harsh on you." She shouldn't have been so hard on Kit without knowing the whole story. People did that to her all the time, and it sucked.

Kit waved a hand. "It's fine. You didn't know."

"Well, I know now." Mona took the third torch from her belt and held it over the fire. It ignited, the three torches giving more light than the two, and she passed it to Kit.

Torpid beamed at her and gave her a wink. Mona ignored him and the fuzzy feeling it gave her and cleared her throat. It was time to get a move on.

"Now," she said, "if there is one thing we can all agree on, it's that we need to stop Boogie. We are all that stands in the way of him hurting Sandman and taking his power. And I don't know about you two, but I don't want to stick around here and find out what he plans to do with that power if he gets it. I don't think it will be easy, but we're the only ones who have a chance of stopping him. But if we're going to do this, we need to be a team. We need to be able to trust that we have each other's backs. No running away when things look bad. We stand together or we don't stand at all. Can you be team players?"

"Yes," said Kit without a slither of sarcasm, holding onto their torch.

"I can be too," said Torpid. He put a clawed hand out between them all and waited expectantly. "How about you, Mona?"

Mona sighed and placed her hand on Torpid's. "I'm in."

They both looked at Kit who joined them, rolling their eyes. Mona caught the hint of a smile that Kit tried hard to cover up.

"Okay, team, let's do this." Torpid gave a whoop and raised their hands into the air like they were about to play a game of basketball. Mona giggled.

"All right, first we need to find a way out of the cave," said Mona.

Kit took a few steps forward into the shadow. "There must be another opening somewhere."

"Uh, Mona," said Torpid, tugging at her hoodie.

"Just a sec," she said, turning back to Kit. "There has to be. It's our only way out short of scaling those cliffs."

Kit played with their red tie. "But how are we going to find it, if there even is another opening? There's no telling how far this cave goes."

Mona grabbed a stick and scratched it along the dirt on the floor, using her torch to highlight her sketch. "We could treat it like a maze. If we follow along one side of the wall, then it should eventually lead us to the exit."

"Mona," repeated Torpid, his voice now a high-pitched squeak.

"What?"

His eyes were as wide as tea plates. "This cave has sp-sp-sp-spiders."

Mona sniggered. "Big whoop, there were a ton of spiders back at the orphanage."

Torpid shook his head. "Not this big."

Mona followed Torpid's gaze to the roof of the cave. She raised her torch to get a better look and was met with dozens of eyes staring down at them, all belonging to the biggest spiders Mona had ever seen.

17

EIGHT-LEGGED FREAKS

*E*ight long, hairy legs, two twitching fangs, eight hungry eyes on each. All of them staring down from the ceiling.

As one they shook their bulbous abdomens and their skin glowed a radioactive green, like night-lights glowing in the cave, only they were the nightmares too.

Mona backed up, unable to tell if Kit's and Torpid's faces were green from the light or green from sickening fear at what hung above them.

"Mona," Torpid half whispered, half shrieked. "What do we do?"

Mona bent down, never taking her eyes from the monsters above, and reached out. Her hand gripped around a thick branch poking out from the edge of the fire. "Run!"

Taking the branch, Mona threw it to the ceiling and straight at the spiders. They hissed, but Mona didn't stick around to see if she struck any of them.

As one, Mona, Torpid, and Kit pelted for the cave mouth. Her heart rattled in her chest and drummed in her ears.

They were almost there, when three of the huge spiders dropped to the ground on silk threads and blocked their path.

Mona stopped, skidding her Converse in the dirt, and grabbed Torpid by the arm, dragging him back just before one of the spiders lunged at him. She jabbed out at it with her torch, but the other two stepped toward them from either side, a full head and shoulders taller than her, clicking at each other in some language she couldn't speak. The meaning was clear enough: Get them.

Scuttling sounded above as more of the arachnids closed in. The three of them ran the other way, into the belly of the cave and the unknown where everything was black.

Mona stole a glance over her shoulder and saw the spiders close behind, their skin illuminating as they charged along the ceiling, ground, and walls like a plague coming to get them.

The cave veered to the left, and they followed it, nowhere else to go, the stampede of spiders at their heels. The green glow reached out over the cave walls before them, growing brighter and brighter with each step.

The spiders were getting closer. They were too fast, their eight legs moving quicker than Mona's two quivering ones could.

They reached a break in the cave and two tunnels branched farther underground, left and right.

"Which way?" asked Kit, their breath labored.

Mona looked to each one, back and forth. They were both too dark to see into. Anything could lay beyond. The glow behind them grew greater still, and Mona could practically feel the spiders crawling over her skin.

"Left!" she called, and the three of them took the turn.

It was the wrong decision.

Mona led the way, her torch raised with the others right behind her. Ten yards into the darkness, her foot stepped out into nothing but air. She tried to stop herself, but Torpid ran into the back of her, then Kit. All of them toppled forward and the wind rushed through Mona's hair as they slid down into shadow.

Their screams echoed through the cave as they plunged into the deep, dark depths below.

They fell forever until the incline stopped and Mona felt herself glide into the air before falling to dirt packed ground with a humph. A pain shot through her butt at the landing and then Torpid and Kit crashed into her in a pile of tangled legs and arms.

An elbow dug into Mona's side, and she tossed and turned to wriggle free from the jumble of limbs, rubbing at a scuff on her leg where a hole had been ripped through her jeans.

Their torches lay on the ground, still burning, but not as bright as before, the flames dying from having consumed most of the wood. Mona picked one up. "Are you two okay?"

"I'm not dead," replied Kit, dusting dirt from their shirt.

"I'm okay," said Torpid. "Are you?"

Mona got to her feet and groaned, stretching her muscles. "Yeah, bumped and scraped, but all good considering."

Their voices echoed, like they were in a large, empty building. Mona walked around, straining her eyes to make anything out.

"What's that noise?" whispered Kit.

Mona listened. A rushing sound. She stepped forward and her shoe hit a puddle. Water hit her head in a drip and she looked up. "It's water. I think this part of the cave is under the lake."

It would explain the moss on the walls and the damp smell. No, it wasn't moss. At least not all of it.

Mona inched closer to the wall and ran her hand over it. It wasn't wet or slimy to the touch.

Mona pulled her hand back as realization kicked in like a blow to the stomach. Wisps of it stuck to her fingers and palm like tendrils of clawing smoke. Cobwebs.

Kit and Torpid came up behind her with their torches and the extra light illuminated the wall. The whole thing was covered in cobwebs. They carried all the way up to the roof of the cave, thick and over-grown like weeds in an abandoned garden.

Mona was right. It was a large room. They stood at the bottom of a deep cavern, stalactites dripping down from the ceiling like stone icicles. Huge webs had been spun between them, the silk glinting gently from the green light.

Green light.

"They're back," warned Mona. The three of them pressed their backs together in a triangle, each keeping watch at different ends of the round cavern.

The light intensified and the nest of spiders spilled out from a hole above and spread through the webs hanging from the ceiling.

There were more now than before. Mona lost count at twenty, her mouth dry and feet ready to run. But there was nowhere to go. They were trapped.

Kit reached out and squeezed Mona's free hand,

their eyes glued to the spiders crawling above. Torpid trembled against her side, the flame of his torch shaking.

The spiders clicked at each other in their spine-chilling method of communication and began to crawl down the webbed walls toward them.

Mona used the glow from their bodies to get a better look at their surroundings. Some spiders moved into holes near the ceiling and their green glow vanished. A few moments later, they returned, coming back into view at the bottom of the cavern through the mouths of tunnels, their reflections distorting in puddles as they stomped their long legs through them to get to their next meal.

But Mona wasn't going to let herself end up on the menu.

"I have an idea," she said, running it through her head. It could work. It had to. She turned to Kit. "Can I trust you?"

"What?" asked Kit, unable to tear their eyes from the approaching doom.

"Can I trust you?" Mona repeated, stepping in front of Kit to meet them in the eyes.

Kit nodded, their face serious. "Yes."

Mona would have to take Kit's word for it and hope they wouldn't run off again. Her plan would need them all.

"Split up," she said, pointing to the tunnel openings in the ceiling as the spiders grew closer. "We climb up the webs, each take a tunnel, and loop back down to the cavern. We need to get all the spiders in the middle of the cavern at the same time."

Torpid gulped. "Then what?"

Mona grinned despite herself. They needed to believe she knew what she was doing. That she had a fool-proof plan and that they'd come out of this still breathing. Even if the odds were super slim. "You'll see."

Torpid held out his hand between them. Kit placed theirs on top. Mona joined them and Torpid raised their hands in the air. "Go, team," he said, setting his jaw and then dashing to the nearest section of the round wall to begin his ascent.

Kit went next, running across the cavern and jumping on the first cobweb leading all the way up to the tunnel opening. Mona wasted no time, and took the section in between Torpid and Kit, treating the webs like ropes on a jungle gym.

The spiders clicked from below and split into three groups, spanning out over the cavern and giving chase.

Torpid was fast, scampering up the webbed wall in no time with agile hands and feet.

Kit wasn't as quick, but their long legs helped to

scale up the connected cobwebs in three or four steps each.

Mona turned her focus to her own climb. The cobwebs were sticky and clung to her clothes like chewing gum. Unlike Kit and Torpid who had abandoned their torches on the floor, Mona had kept hers, the idea of losing sight of her surroundings too scary. It was slowing her down.

The webs rattled from the weight of her pursuers below. Five massive arachnids with twitching fangs headed her way on legs perfectly suited to the silken cobwebs they had built. Their glow made her torch seem useless now, but she couldn't let it go. What if they turned their lights off like they had done at the cave mouth? None of them knew the spiders were there, carrying out a sneak attack, until it was too late.

"Mona!" shouted Kit from across the cavern.

Mona looked down just in time to see the fangs of one of the spiders snap at her ankle. She moved it away in the nick of time, the fangs sinking into the wall.

The spider hissed in fury and made to attack her again.

Mona kicked out and hit it in the face. It recoiled and Mona tried to climb away.

The web shook below her again, stronger this time, as the others caught up with the spider leading the way.

Mona lost her grip, her hand holding the torch slipping. Her feet wobbled under the strain and lost their hold too.

Mona screamed and held on with one arm, hanging like a worm on a hook.

Her shoulder ached under her own weight, her muscles straining and unused to bearing such a load.

The spiders saw their opportunity and set in toward her.

Mona's frantic feet found purchase, the stickiness of the cobwebs coming in handy. She threw her left arm toward the wall and it stuck too, holding her in place, torch still tight in her grasp.

The torch brushed the cobwebs around it and the silk shriveled at the touch of the flames, like cotton candy caught in the rain. It broke apart the surrounding cobwebs, creating a hole in the structure.

Mona laughed, giddy and terrified at the same time.

Another spider lurched toward her, but Mona was ready for it this time. She gripped onto the web with one arm and swiped the torch around her with the other, making sure to touch the silk the whole way.

Like before, the cobwebs shriveled and disintegrated, only this time it was on a much larger scale.

The weight of the spiders was too much for the burned web to handle. The holes from the fire opened and ripped under the added strain of the five eight-legged freaks who were after her, and they flopped back on themselves, creating big gaps in the wall and sending all five of the spiders crashing to the ground.

"Take that, you bunch of googly eyed creeps!"

Mona would have hung there and sent more taunts their way, but the spiders regrouped below her and began to scale the wall again. Their route was longer thanks to the fire, but they edged around it in a wide berth and zeroed in on her from each side.

Ignoring the excited clacking and hissing, Mona surged on, not daring to look back until she reached the top. Her body wailed as fatigue set in, but she couldn't stop. She had seen what spiders did to flies caught in their webs.

Finally, she reached the opening of the tunnel and tossed her torch through it, throwing a leg over the edge and hoisting herself up. She risked a look down and saw the spiders close behind, close enough to see the saliva escaping their mouths.

Mona got to her feet and ran, sweat beading on her forehead. The green glow joined her soon after, the shadows of the spiders on the walls like moving hieroglyphics. She threw the torch behind her, any delays in their advance worth the possible loss of light, and stomped down through the tunnel.

She reached the bottom and headed for the center

of the cavern. Kit and Torpid headed toward her from opposite ends, spiders on each of their tails. Mona dug into the pouches on her belt as she ran, allowing her instincts to select the colors.

The trio met in the middle of the cavern. The spiders charged for them from all corners, circling them in victory.

"Whatever you're planning to do, now would be a good time to do it," rasped Kit, doubled over with hands on their knees.

Mona held out the pile of sand before her. She took a deep breath and focused, brushing away the welling fear inside her as she thought about Torpid and his dream. A pool at the bottom of a waterfall. The sound of rushing water as it plummeted from above. The feeling of water touching her skin, wet and cool.

The sand changed in her hand and she opened her eyes to see a ball of water hover above her palm. It rose, higher and higher into the air, growing bigger the farther it went. Mona asked the sand to work faster, willed it with all her might, and the sphere of liquid shot up like a cannonball and collided with the rock surface of the ceiling.

There was a moment of silence before chaos erupted.

A grumbling came from above like the roar of a sleeping giant who'd been woken up well before his alarm went off. The whole cavern began to quake, sending vibrations through the walls, over the ground, and up Mona's already-shaking legs. Even the spiders moved their attention to the ceiling, their dinner forgotten with the rumbling tremors coursing through the cave.

The stalactites shook and cracks split down them. They broke off into jagged shards and fell to the ground in spears. Mona, Kit, and Torpid nudged close to each other and shrieks filled the room.

The ceiling crumbled and fell in spears, squishing some of the spiders and crushing them into nothing but splats of bright green goo.

Then the water came.

It ripped through the ceiling and burst out from the cracks like a busted city fire hydrant in the summer.

Her plan had worked.

It had worked too well.

Mona jerked her two companions back and, amid the confusion, weaved through the spiders toward an opening across the cavern, dodging pieces of fallen debris and clusters of rock.

The water rained down in a crashing wave. The tsunami barged in through the hole in the ceiling like water spiraling down a sink drain, only on a much larger scale.

The spiders clicked frantically to each other before

the water met them and their chatter turned to ear-splitting shrieks and gurgled hissing.

The spiders on the periphery ran toward the tunnel opening where Mona had led Kit and Torpid. Water ran past their feet, brushing their ankles and soaking their shoes, shallow but rising with great speed as more and more water filled the cavern.

Flashes of the lake danced in Mona's mind. Of gasping for air with burning lungs, of sinking deep underwater.

Torpid took her hand, Kit taking the other, breaking her out of her panic. They urged her forward, into the tunnel and away from the water that chased them.

Spiders ran behind them, slipping in the surging water and running over each other in a bid to get away.

The water was up to Mona's knees now. Kit grabbed Torpid whose chest was submerged and hoisted him onto their back.

The water was rising too fast. They'd never make it.

A spider whizzed by them, curled into a ball and spitting, swept away by the flow. They had escaped one peril and dove straight into another.

Then she thought of it.

As she ran, Kit by her side and Torpid holding

onto their neck, she grabbed sand from the pouch and thought back to what Torpid told her about his dream. He had been in the pool by the waterfall relaxing. In the water, floating.

Mona sent her intentions to the sand, their last hope of making it out of there. The sand glittered pink and separated into three mounds. They grew and shaped themselves into rings, expanding in a sound like that of blowing up a balloon.

The sand solidified and three oddly shaped inflatable rings appeared. They were more oval than perfect rings, and, like the dolphins, they never switched from glittering sand to the actual look of the object, but Mona didn't care.

Kit took a ring and jumped onto it, Torpid hopping from their back onto the second one as Mona took her seat on the third. The water collected the rings immediately and sent them all shooting down the cave in a rush of crashing waves.

The spiders had stopped their shrieking behind them, a green glow whizzing by underwater here and there as they swept down the tunnel in a river-rapids course, heading through the cave's network of tunnels.

The farther they were carried, the higher the water got. The cave veered right and Mona had to lean all her weight to one side of the ring to avoid colliding with the solid walls.

Kit and Torpid bobbed along beside her, holding on as best they could and mirroring her at shifting their weight, like they were all riding high-speed motorbikes.

Mona wished she had a helmet.

She looked across to Kit and the water was now so high, they had to duck their head from hitting the tunnel roof.

The rushing waves picked up speed, hurtling them through so fast, Mona couldn't control the ring. The three of them careened through, unable to do anything but try to stay afloat.

The tunnel dipped and Mona bounced from the impact, slipping in her seat, the rubber slick from the water. They funneled into a small room and her heart sank.

The tunnel just stopped. There was no connecting route, no way out. Nothing. Nothing but the water that swirled under them upon meeting the dead end.

"We're done for," cried Torpid as the water filled the room and raised them higher.

Mona closed her eyes.

"I don't know about that," said Kit. Mona snapped her eyes open and followed where Kit pointed above them.

An opening. It was right above them, and the water was propelling them straight for it like a cannon.

"Hold on!" yelled Mona, and she braced herself.

One second she was in the cave, and the next she was shooting out into open air, the water bursting out from underground like it was shooting through a whale's blowhole.

All three of them landed with a bounce as the rubber rings met the ground, water from the spurting hole raining down on them.

Mona looked at her companions and they broke into a bout of uncontrollable laughter, a blend of relief and pure joy, singing in the rain.

18

THE HAUNTED HOUSE

*D*ripping wet, Mona, Kit, and Torpid trudged away from the hole in the cave they shot out of, the water still spurting from it like a park fountain.

Their shoes squished with each step and the cold swept past them in a constant chill, but things could have been worse. A lot worse. The still-trapped-in-a-cave-with-a-nest-of-spiders kind of worse.

The abrupt exit from the cave had brought them to a barren field, nothing but dried-up bushes snagging their ankles with thorns like claws.

"The tunnels must have led us past the cliff," said Mona. The lake was far off in the distance now, black as night. They all turned to face what lay ahead.

"Well, nothing for it but to keep on moving forward," said Torpid. He took a couple steps down the path before tripping over a branch and landing on his face.

Mona and Kit suppressed their sniggers and helped the sloth up.

"Whoops," said Torpid, spitting out a mouthful of dirt.

"Thanks for having our backs down there, Kit," said Mona.

"I guess we're a team now, or whatever," replied Kit, looking at their feet and scratching the back of their neck.

"You betcha," said Torpid, giving them a warm smile.

A team. Mona wasn't on any teams. Extracurricular activities only meant more time at school, and a lot of them cost money for uniforms or equipment. At Ms. Gloomberg's, it was every kid for themselves. Besides, she was better off alone. Relying on other people only led to disappointment.

Then again, if Torpid hadn't been there to tell her how to use the sand, she could have been captured by the circus clowns, or ended up in the belly of the sea monster.

If Kit hadn't warned her about the spider lunging toward her, she could have been trapped on a web, cocooned inside like a fly until the nest decided which of them got to enjoy her for supper.

Maybe being on a team had its good points. Maybe.

They carried on through the field, weaving between the overgrown bushes and helping each other when they stumbled or got their clothes caught in the thorns. The farther they went, the thicker and taller the bushes got, so much so they couldn't see beyond the next overgrowth in front of them.

Despite this, there was a spring in Mona's step, and she couldn't quite figure out why. It wasn't like they had found Sandman or defeated Boogie. They didn't even know if they were headed in the right direction. Nevertheless, she felt better than she had since the whole mess began, lighter somehow.

"You know," she said, holding a rather nasty-looking branch out of the way for Kit and Torpid to pass, "I think we might just be able to do this."

"Of course we can," said Torpid, ducking under the branch. "Sandman always says that if you want something, all you have to do is work hard and believe you can accomplish your goal."

Kit rolled their eyes and followed behind the sloth. "Sandman sounds like a self-help book."

Mona went last and carefully let go of the branch so it didn't come back to swat her in the face with its razor-sharp thorns. Kit and Torpid had stopped walking. She was about to ask why when she saw it.

Directly in front of them, surrounded by the forest of ensnaring bushes, lay a house.

Easily ten times the size of the orphanage, it towered over them like a school bully after their lunch money. Its windows glared down at them with menacing eyes, the large arched doorway frowning at their arrival.

None of them moved any closer. The walls were gray, just like Boogie's skin, and a gang of gargoyles watched with moving eyes from their perch on the jagged roof, their faces held in eternal torment.

Torpid let out an audible gulp. "I wonder what's inside."

"Whatever it is, it can't be worse than bedbugs, horror movie clowns, slimy sea monsters, or a nest of human-eating spiders," said Mona.

Kit shook their head. "Why does everything in this land want to eat us?"

"Maybe they like the taste of people," ventured Torpid.

Kit considered this and said, "Well, I do look delicious."

Mona nudged Kit in the ribs. "Careful, or your big head won't fit through the door."

"We're going in, then?" asked Torpid.

"There's no other way through," said Kit, glancing around. "The bushes surround the whole front of the house, and I don't think we'll get much farther trying to sneak between these." Kit kicked at the bush next to them, the stems and branches thick as tree trunks.

"We can do this," said Mona, more to herself than her companions. "All we have to do is open the door and walk inside."

"Sure," agreed Kit. "It's getting back out that will be the problem."

"Have you considered a career in motivational speaking?" asked Mona.

"I'm sorry, what I meant to say was," Kit cleared their throat and gave their best Sandman impression, "just believe and you can accomplish your dreams, or something."

"That's the spirit," said Torpid.

Mona suppressed a laugh and stepped forward. The longer they stood there putting it off, the more intimidating it got. Bold as brass, Mona took the stone stairs, reached the door, and yanked it open. "Come on," she said, hoping they missed the shake in her voice.

If they caught it, neither of them said anything. Instead, they marched up the steps to meet her and walked across the threshold, side by side like any good team should.

As soon as they were through, the door slammed shut with a bang. Torpid grabbed at the handle and pulled. "It's locked," he squeaked.

"That's okay," said Mona, her nails digging into her palms. "We just need to find the back door. That's all."

Kit examined the room with their hands on their hips. "Then we better start looking, because this is one creepy house."

It was more of a mansion, really, though not like the kind Mona had seen on TV, with their bright white walls and big windows to let the light shine through. This was like the home of Count Dracula.

Purple, moth-eaten curtains draped the windows, blocking out any light from outside. Not that there was much light to keep out given where they were.

Candles lined the walls in a dull glow, creating shadows over the creaking wood floors and leaving the corners in pure darkness.

Somewhere in the house, a piano was playing. It sang a haunted, out-of-tune melody that echoed through the rooms like the wails of a mourner at a funeral and caused the hairs on Mona's arms to stand on end.

Torpid shook like someone had just walked over his grave. "This place gives me the heebie-jeebies."

Mona zipped up her hoodie and shifted her eyes

over the house. "Yeah, it's creepy all right." The foyer was large, like a gothic cathedral, and their whispers carried. A huge candelabra hung from the ceiling and rocked back and forth of its own accord, the rusted chain holding it creaking in a metallic whine.

A twin set of stairs curved up to the second floor directly in front of them, covered in a bloodred carpeting. At either side of the foyer lay long, narrow corridors, both lined with rows of knights in jagged armor, grasping long swords and maces.

Mona's ears pricked and she eyed the top of the stairs. Voices carried down from somewhere above, and they were getting closer.

"Someone's coming," she said, grabbing Kit and Torpid. "Quick, hide."

They tiptoed to the left corridor and scurried around to the back of a particularly large knight. From the height and width of the thing, the armor had been fashioned for a giant.

Mona made a mental note not to climb any beanstalks if they happened across one, and crouched as low as she could, the three of them slipping into the darkness of the knight's vast shadow.

"What is it?" Torpid asked, eyes covered with both clawed hands.

"Sshhh," warned Mona, putting a finger to Torpid's lips. She peered around the legs of the giant knight and waited on the balls of her feet as the voices grew louder and in number. Four or five people at least, from what she could hear.

Mona felt Kit stiffen behind her as the owners of the voices came into view.

"You don't think this place has a phone, do you?" Kit whispered in her ear. "I think we need to call the Ghostbusters."

Ten people descended the staircase. Or, to be exact, they glided down a couple inches in the air above each step. All were ghostly pale, for that was what they were: ghosts.

Like a hologram, each of the figures was transparent. There, but not there. They floated down to the foyer, all dressed in shabby rags that hung down to where their knees should've been.

All of them were human, and all of them were unhappy. Furious was more like it. Accusing fingers stabbed in the air as they talked over each other in a babble of anger and frustration.

"What's going on?" asked Torpid, peeking through his fingers.

"They're arguing," said Kit, their head leaning over Mona's shoulder for a better look.

The adults faced off against each other, yelling and squabbling over who knows what. Whatever it was, it was heated.

"Let's get out of here while we can," said Mona, standing. The ghosts were their own perfect distraction, too wrapped up in their fight to notice Mona, Kit, and Torpid slipping down the corridor.

Kit nodded and followed, poking Torpid in the side to get his attention. Torpid, eyes covered, felt the poke and yelped in fright, like he thought it was one of the ghosts coming for him. He sprang up from his curled position on the floor and fell back against the giant knight.

The knight wobbled from the impact. Mona dove toward it, but she was too late. The metal helmet at the top of the armor jerked forward on its neck before it fell to the floor with a clattering crash.

"Uh-oh," said Torpid, slowly looking behind him to see all the ghosts staring at them, their argument forgotten.

Mona inched back. "Now would be a good time to run."

"On three?" asked Kit, watching the ghosts like they were a bunch of wild animals ready to pounce.

"Let's skip the countdown," said Mona. As one, the threesome darted off like they were at the Olympics and shooting for gold on the race track.

The ghosts howled behind them and a gust of wind swept through the corridor, propelling them forward and away from the foyer. The knights rattled in fear from the cries, armor barely holding together.

Mona bounded down, the hood of her jacket flapping up over her head like a tornado was fast approaching and almost at her heels. She risked a glance back and was met with the gang of ghouls flying in their direction.

They were arguing again, even as they gave chase, their faces haunted masks of fury and outrage.

"They're going to catch us," panted Kit.

Mona reached for her belt of sand, but before she even had time to undo one of the pouches, the ghosts were on them. They rocketed straight at them with inhuman speed.

Mona raised her arms in defense and braced herself for impact.

The ghosts careened forward, but instead of smashing against Mona and her friends, the ghosts passed right through their bodies.

An arctic freeze zipped through Mona's body upon contact, like shards of ice each time one of the ghosts passed through her. It stopped her in her tracks, the breath sweeping from her lungs in the shock of the cold.

Kit fell to their knees beside her and gasped, Torpid not doing much better.

The ghosts whirled around behind them with sinister faces and cackled in a choir of the dead. Their voices reverberated off the walls and through the corridor, evil laughter escaping their blue lips. As a group, they turned in the air and flew off down the corridor, the laughing ringing in Mona's ears like an emergency siren.

Mona watched the ghosts until they were gone, her temper rising. She set her jaw, blood boiling in a wave of rage that seemed to have come from nowhere and all at once.

She tapped her foot on the ground, arms crossed and fingers itching to grab a fistful of sand and take off after the ghosts to show them who they were dealing with.

"I feel funny," groaned Torpid, his eyebrows furrowed to meet at the top of his nose. A frown didn't look right on him, like a piece of a jigsaw puzzle accidentally placed in the wrong position.

"Me too," said Mona, her tone sharp even to her own ears, though she didn't understand why. Something had come over her as soon as the ghost passed through her.

Kit got up from the floor and shook their head in clear disapproval. "Don't you get it? The ghosts were all angry and now suddenly we are, stupid. They've done something to us. Talk about obvious."

Mona pulled her head back and regarded Kit. "No need to snap, jerk face." She took a step toward them.

"No need to call me jerk face, jerk face," Kit retorted, getting in her personal space.

Torpid stood between them and pushed them apart, harder than necessary. "Stop going at each other. I hate it when you do that. It's very annoying."

Kit snorted at the sloth. "If you hadn't been such a klutz, this wouldn't have happened. But no, you had to freak out at the tiniest little thing and give us away. Great job, Weird Hairy Guy. Helpful as ever."

"I've helped," snapped Torpid, his fur standing up. "Mona would still be trying to conjure monsters if it weren't for me."

"Shut up, both of you," injected Mona, pinching her nose at the sound of their voices. They went right through her. "And Torpid, I would have figured how to use the sand on my own. I'm not a complete idiot."

Kit made a face. "I don't know about that."

"What have you done? Huh?" Torpid demanded of Kit while he balled his hands into fists. "Nothing, that's what. I tried to warn you, Mona. You wouldn't listen. Kit can't be trusted. They say they don't work for Boogie, but how do we know they're telling the truth?"

"You think I care if you believe me? Dream on."

Kit turned to Mona. "I don't even know why you brought him with us. All he does is get in the way."

Torpid thumped a thumb on his chest. "At least I am a team player."

Mona threw her hands up and swiped the air. "Look at us! We aren't a team. I don't do teams, and if I did, I certainly wouldn't choose a hyperactive sloth who's scared to leave the house, or some woe-is-me, pity-partying goth kid."

"Pity-partying?" asked Kit, eyes dark.

Mona put on the voice of a whiny toddler and mimicked rubbing her eyes. "Oh, poor me. Boogie threatened my family and took me away. Wah, wah, wah. At least you have a family."

"Don't talk about my family," shouted Kit, their face red.

Mona looked Kit up and down like they were nothing. "I'll talk about what I want."

Torpid was still on his rant while Mona and Kit exchanged words. "And for all we know," said the sloth, "they helped Boogie escape in the first place."

"Wrong," said Kit. "Again. Maybe you should try looking at the other member of this stupid little team." Kit shot a pointed glare at Mona.

Torpid drew his attention to her. "What do they mean? Mona?" Understanding lit in his eyes. "You didn't?"

"Well, you see—" stumbled Mona, searching for the right words.

Torpid's mouth dropped open. "You did!"

"Told you it wasn't me," said Kit.

Mona turned on him. "Shut up, Kit," she said, tempted to sock them in the face for what they just spilled.

"You shut up. I told you not to open the door, but you did it anyway."

"You lied to me," said Torpid through gritted teeth, like the sloth was about to lose his cool big time.

"I tried to tell you." Mona huffed. "And I didn't lie. I withheld the truth. There's a clear difference."

Torpid's face was bitter, like he'd drunk a bottle of vinegar and the taste still lingered. "Boogie got out because of you. Sandman's life is in danger because of you. He is the last Dream Weaver, the only one left to keep the dreams of everyone alive. This is all your fault."

"Torpid, I—"

"No," he snapped, raising a palm at her to stop. "You can't be trusted. I'll find Sandman on my own." And with that, Torpid left, stomping down the corridor where the ghosts had gone. He didn't look back once.

"Fine," Mona called to Torpid's back.

"Looks like the band has broken up," said Kit with a sneer.

Mona pushed the nearest knight that stood next to her and sent it to the floor where it broke into its individual parts with a crash. "Why did you tell him?"

"Why didn't you?" asked Kit, kicking a bit of the armor away that landed near their boots.

"Because I didn't want to complicate things." Why did Kit need to open their big mouth? She should have left them back on the Sanctuary and in the prison cell where they belonged.

"You mean, you didn't want him to know you ruined things."

Mona released the frustrated grumble festering in her throat. Kit was infuriating and they just wouldn't stop talking. Ever. "You think you're so smart, but you're just a scared little kid."

"I'm not going to argue with you anymore," said Kit, like they were somehow the bigger person. "You're not worth it. But what I am doing is walking away. You're on your own."

Kit walked off in the opposite direction and headed down the other corridor to the right of the foyer.

"Good!" she shouted. "I'm better off alone anyway. You and Torpid were only slowing me down."

Mona kicked at the armor and stubbed her toe on a solid piece of metal on the chest piece. "Ouch," she yelled, which turned into a scream. She kicked another piece on the way to the foyer and looked around the room.

No way was she going down either corridor. She never wanted to see Kit's or Torpid's faces again. Not in this life, and not in the afterlife if she ever ended up like one of those dumb ghosts. She didn't need them. She'd never needed anyone before, so as far as she was concerned, things were better this way. Much better.

Mona stomped up the staircase. Dust-covered curtains draped over a large window at the top. She grabbed each end of the curtains and threw them back to get a good look at what waited for them outside in the hopes that the garden would give away where the back door was located.

Out back was unlike any garden Mona had ever seen in the city, that was for sure. It stretched out forever, dark green hedges high and shaped into walls that weaved in an intricate pattern, round and round, jutting off here and there, stopping in places and winding down closer to the center in others.

"A maze," she said, her breath frosting the window.

Mona focused her attention on the middle of the labyrinth and gasped. It was definitely the same place. A domed podium sat in the center of the maze, stairs leading up to it and spiraled stone pillars holding it up. Mounds of black piled on the stairs as well as inside the podium floor.

It was the place from her dream, from the nightmare she had after Boogie blew black sand in her face. The same black sand that was all over the podium where he had stood and addressed his army of hideous bedbugs.

Mona shivered at the thought of the vile creatures. She even thought she'd seen a glimpse of them in the window, her tired, angry mind playing tricks on her. She gave herself a shake and squeezed her eyes shut and opened them again.

She started. The bugs were still there, in the window.

Before Mona could react to the reflection staring back at her, the bedbugs grabbed her from behind. Something hit her on the back of the head and everything went black.

19
LOST FAMILY

*B*lack *sand swirled around Mona like a tornado.*
She was trapped in the heart of it, unable to see or
break out from its clutches.

It circled around her, growing faster and more violent. Then, all at once, the sand stopped. It danced away from her into the night like it was being sucked up in a vacuum to reveal her location.

She wasn't in the mansion anymore. The bedbugs were nowhere to be seen.

Mona took a step forward, her muscles taut and body ready to fight, flee, or freak out. She wasn't sure which.

"It's a dream," she told herself, taking a deep, calming breath. In and out. It was only a dream. One of Boogie's lingering nightmares, thanks to his sand.

Still, her reassurances did little to calm her thumping heart.

Mona found herself in a cottage, warm and inviting with a fire crackling in the corner, illuminating everything in a comfortable light. Trees with vibrant green leaves peeked in through the windows, a river flowing past and down the glen. It was a far cry from the Land of Nightmares.

A plump sofa was positioned before the flames, and a woman sat there with her bare feet resting on a wooden coffee table. Her long, silken hair draped over her shoulders, hands resting over a protruding baby bump. She radiated happiness, wearing it like a favorite coat.

"Here you go," said a man's voice. Mona turned toward it and almost fell back as she lay eyes on Boogie. She scurried to move out of his way, breath trapped in her throat even though it was a dream. He had seen her there, in her nightmare, the first time when he was addressing his bugs, but this Boogie continued straight past her toward the woman on the sofa.

"Careful," he said, handing a steaming mug to her, "it's hot."

The woman wrapped her hands around the mug and reached her head up to kiss Boogie. His irises were brown, yet unmarked by evil, and he only had eyes for the woman. She took a sip of the tea and sat back, letting out a contented sigh.

Boogie ran a hand over the bump and smiled, not one of the sinister grins that haunted Mona's dreams, but a true smile. One of joy.

"Not long now," said the woman.

Boogie kissed her on the head. "I love you, Katherine." A chain swung on his neck as he leaned forward, holding a crescent-moon-shaped glass vial filled with golden sand.

"I love you too," said Katherine, rubbing her hand over his and the bump.

Boogie straightened up and crossed the room to where a pile of wood shavings dusted the floor, next to a beautiful handcrafted crib.

Mona inched forward for a better look, quite certain Boogie couldn't see her. He sat down and picked up a half-finished headboard, carving into it with a chisel, his fingers precise as he worked on a design with rainbows and a unicorn.

Mona eyed the finished crib, noting the headboard with a phoenix rising from the ashes carved into it, and then looked back to Boogie. Then it dawned on her.

Boogie and Katherine were expecting twins.

A swooshing sound filled the cottage and the black sand returned. It wrapped around Mona and wiped the picture before her away like an Etch A Sketch.

The sand dissipated after a while and Mona tried to get her bearings, stumbling into something next to her. Her hands clenched around smooth wood and she peered down to see she was clutching a sanded-down corner of a crib. It rocked from side to side at her touch next to the now-finished second crib, the unicorn skipping mid-prance on the headboard under a rainbow. Boogie had put a lot of work into them, the images so detailed and intricate.

It was bright outside, the sun shining through the windows with the sounds of birds singing their morning songs. But the mood inside the cottage told of a more somber day.

A cough came from down the hall. Mona left the living area and followed the coughing as it grew in intensity, a series of hacking croaks that made her own throat itch.

A door lay ajar at the bottom of the hall, and Mona stuck her head inside.

Katherine lay in bed and Mona startled at the sight of her. Her radiance had diminished, like a wilting flower that was once in full bloom. Her cheeks were sunken and bags hung under her eyes like she hadn't slept in days.

Boogie sat on the edge of the bed, his big hands caressing one of Katherine's like he was handling a glass sculpture, gentle as if his mere touch might break her. Their matching rings glinted in the sun coming through the bedroom window.

Katherine shivered as the coughing gave way and Boogie pulled the blanket over her and tucked her in. He didn't look much better than his wife. He watched her like a hawk, scanning her face and wincing every time she coughed.

Katherine's body jerked with each fit of coughing, her body curling in on itself beneath the sheets.

Mona sat down at the opposite side of the bed and ran a hand down the side of Katherine's sweating face. Her fingers passed right through the woman.

"Can I get you anything?" asked Boogie.

Mona paid attention to his face. If Katherine asked him for the world, he would've brought it to her in a box. He would do anything for her, that much was clear. Anything for her and his unborn children.

Katherine gave Boogie a smile, her eyes betraying the effort even that small gesture took her. "No, my love. I just need to rest."

The sand returned and this time Mona tried to outrun it. She wanted to stay and watch over poor Katherine. But it was no use. The black sand brushed over the surroundings once again and, like before, Mona found herself fast-forwarded in time.

It was nighttime now, and the cottage was dark. A full moon hung in the sky between the trees, making everything appear cold and hollow. The cribs were still there, waiting for the arrival of the babies. The rest of the living area was disheveled and unkempt, unfinished plates of food sitting by the kitchen sink, a vase of dead flowers, dried and brittle leaves fallen around the outside of the base like ashes, zapped of color and life.

Mona made to return to the bedroom, trepidation building in her chest. A pained noise slipped through the cottage and she hurried, rushing so fast she walked straight into Boogie. He passed right through her like she was one of the ghosts back at the mansion, and he paced, up and down the hall, wringing his hands and running shaking fingers through his hair.

There were more cries, and they didn't belong to a baby. Mona reached for the handle of the bedroom door, but her hand went right through it. She cursed.

And then the cries stopped.

The silence loomed over the hallway, loud and unbearable.

Boogie stopped his pacing and stood still like he was frozen in place, body rigid. He made for the door in three long strides.

The bedroom door opened before he reached it. A woman came out, face pale, a doctor's bag in her hand.

"Is she okay?" Boogie asked, his whole face collapsed like he already knew the answer. Like he felt it deep within him that his world had irreparably changed forever.

The doctor shook her head, her voice soft. "There was nothing I could do."

Boogie's face crumpled. "And the babies?"

The doctor hung her head. "I'm sorry."

Boogie fell to his knees like a broken marionette whose strings had been cut off. The sound of his heart breaking was almost audible, like a crack of thunder, his despair palpable, static in the air. He leaned back, tears running down his anguished face, and let out an earth-shattering scream into the night.

20
LOCKED UP

ona came crashing back to reality.
Literally.

She landed smack down onto a cold stone floor,
face-first, tossed like a bag of garbage. With a groan,
she turned just in time to see the bedbugs who'd
jumped her slam the door shut, their ugly faces smug.

A lock clicked, echoing off the bare stone walls,
soon followed by the raucous laughter of her bug-eyed
captors.

"Oh yeah?" she called to them through the door,
sitting up and wincing at the pain in her arm. "You
jumped me from behind when I wasn't looking. If you
cowards think you're so tough, then come back in here
and fight me, girl to butt-ugly insect."

"I think they're gone," said a voice.

Mona sighed.

"They got you too, then," she said to Kit, her back to them.

"They got us all," came Torpid's voice.

Mona dropped her waving fists and let her arms fall to her side. "Well, that puts a severe damper on my hopes of one of you getting me out of here."

She faced her cellmates. They sat on the dusty floor, looking as glum as she felt, the anger from earlier having vanished, leaving her weak and bone tired.

"I thought we were only slowing you down?" jabbed Kit.

Mona crossed her arms and straightened her back. "You were."

Kit shook their head. "And yet, here you are. Tell me, how is going it alone working out for you?"

"Fine, actually. I can get myself out of here." Mona reached to her belt and the pouches of sand. She'd have the door knocked down in no time and then she could exterminate those oversized pests of Boogie's.

But the pouches weren't there. Her belt was gone.

"They took your belt while you were out. Looks like you're not getting out of here anytime soon." Kit tapped the spot on the floor next to them.

"Shut up, Kit. My head hurts enough as it is." Going by the throbbing at the back of her head, the bedbugs must have hit her hard. She stared at the low ceiling of the tiny, empty room.

Images from her dream circled in her mind. Of Katherine's drawn face, and the painful cries of the man who is now Boogie. The cribs that would never be slept in. The poor unborn babies. It was the worst nightmare yet.

Mona hobbled over to the wall her old companions sat against and plopped herself down with all the grace of an elephant on roller skates.

Torpid bunched along the floor to widen the gap between them.

Mona didn't blame him.

The room grew silent and awkwardness lingered in a dense fog over them all. Mona pulled her legs up to her chest and rested her chin on her knees.

A tiny window looked out into the sky across from her. It was a lot darker than it had been when they'd first entered the mansion. Night had arrived.

From what Mona could tell, they were in one of the mansion's turrets that sprouted from the corners of the roof. The wall circled around either side of the locked door, forcing them into one another's vision whether they liked it or not.

The dust clung to the back of Mona's throat with

every breath, her body tired yet still aching to be out in an open space. The walls pressed down on her, dominant in their confinement. There was no way out.

"I can't believe it ended like this," she said. They'd been doing so well until the ghosts appeared. All that hard work and effort was for nothing. They had failed.

She had failed.

"Poor Sandman," sniffed Torpid, his legs sprawled out in defeat, head slumped.

Mona closed her eyes and rested her head against the stone behind her. Sandman.

What was happening to him right now? Where was he? What was Boogie doing to him? Was he gone, or still hanging on, hoping that someone would come and save him? Now those hopes, all their hopes, were shattered. They had lost to Boogie and his mangy bedbugs.

Kit ran a hand through their black-and-red hair, rocking back and forth. "You have no idea what Boogie is going to do to us."

"Oh, I think I have a good idea." Mona had seen what he did to his enemies. Raya was nothing but sand by the time Boogie finished with her. Her and the rest of the Dream Weavers. Had he done the same to Sandman by now? If not, then it was just a matter of time. Boogie would get what he wanted, and there was nothing anyone could do to stop him now. It was over.

They had lost before they'd even begun. They were

just two kids and a sloth, up against the bringer of nightmares himself. It was a terrible move coming to Boogie's playground, and she had dragged Kit and Torpid down there with her.

Mona hugged her knees tighter. "Who were we even kidding? What good were the three of us going to be standing up against the Boogie Man? If the Dream Weavers couldn't do it, then we were bound to fail from the beginning."

"I'm not going to argue with you on that one," said Kit. "Some team we turned out to be."

"I can't even use the sand right. I would have made a terrible apprentice. Ms. Gloomberg was right about me all along," said Mona, hearing the old director's voice ring in her mind. "I'm no good."

"I'm never going to see my family again." Kit had a far-off look on their face, eyes haunted like they were watching a living nightmare. "Boogie warned me. He told me he'd hurt them if I didn't do what he ordered. And here I am trying to help take him down. They're in real trouble now, and it's all because of me."

Torpid leaned against the wall, limp like an abandoned stuffed toy, lips downturned and reaching for the floor. "If we lose Sandman, then there will be no one left to deliver dreams. All that will be left is Boogie. He'll spread his fear and nightmares to everyone with no one to stop him. All hope will be lost."

The sloth's bottom lip shook. "You were both right. I've been no help. If anything, all I've done is get in the way and slow you down. I should have stayed home."

"You've done really well leaving the Sanctuary after all that time," said Mona.

Torpid looked at her for the first time. Sadness peered out from behind his eyes where joy used to be. Joy that had been taken because of her.

"I had to. Sandman was in trouble. I'd do anything to help him."

Mona gave him a little smile. "That's what makes you an amazing friend."

Kit sighed from across the room. "I should have told you, explained better back on the ship about Boogie being behind the door. I was too busy being a jerk, and now he's out and everything is terrible."

"You did tell me not to open it," said Mona. Kit warned her not to, and she did it anyway. A part of her opened it because Kit had told her not to. No one told her what to do. Or at least when they did, she never listened.

Kit shook their head. "I also lied to you to get out of the cell. You both came here thinking you had a guide, and all I did was try to save my own skin when we were in trouble."

"At first, maybe. But you helped us down in the caves. We might not have made it out of there without your help." Mona refused to allow Kit to place the blame on themselves. This was on her.

Mona stared down at her hands and picked at the dirt under her nails from their travels. "I know I haven't been a good friend. I've never really had any friends, so I guess it's all sort of new to me." She looked up and met each of their eyes, willing them to see she meant every word. "But I messed up and there's no excuse for it. All I can say is that I'm sorry, and I hope you forgive me. I understand if you don't—"

Furry arms wrapped around Mona's neck before she could say anything else. A big weight left her shoulders, and she hugged the sloth back in a tight embrace.

"We all make mistakes," said Torpid in her ear. "It's what we do to fix them that counts."

Mona dropped her hands and bit at her lip. "I tried to fix things, but look where we are. I messed up again."

Torpid picked up her hand and gave it a squeeze. "But you tried. That's what counts."

"And you're not all to blame," said Kit, getting up from their spot on the floor and walking over. "I think it's fair to say we've all messed up. My running away and not helping you both, for one."

"And it was my fault the ghosts heard us," added Torpid.

Mona saw what they were doing, and her heart soared at them for trying. "But none of those things would have happened if I hadn't let Boogie out in the first place."

"Boogie would have gotten out on his own," said Kit, voice firm. "I bet even Sandman knew that he would break free eventually."

"That doesn't excuse what I've done," replied Mona. This was all down to her, no matter what they said. She wouldn't let herself forget that.

Kit bent down on their knees next to her. "It's like Torpid said though. You're trying to make up for it and fix things."

Torpid raised her chin and smiled at her. "Look how far we got. Kit and I couldn't have made it this far without you. I don't think either of us would have even tried."

"And so what if your conjuring doesn't come out perfect?" said Kit. "Your mojo with the sand has saved our butts at every corner. And that's with no training. Imagine how baller you're going to be once you've done your apprenticeship."

Mona thought of the woman with the beaded hair from the portrait on board the Sanctuary—the one who looked like her. All dreams Mona had of being a fierce Dream Weaver were obliterated. "I'll never even start my apprenticeship. Sandman could already be gone, and even if we somehow managed to get out of this mess and save him, he wouldn't want me anywhere near him. And I wouldn't blame him. I wouldn't want me for an apprentice either."

"Okay, enough," said Kit. He patted Torpid on the shoulder "I'm taking a leaf out of my guy Torpid's book and trying to be positive. No more shoulda-woulda-couldas, ifs, buts, or maybes. What's done is done, and all we can do is keep moving forward, right?"

Mona grinned despite herself. "Now who sounds like a self-help book?"

"Ha, ha," said Kit. "But I'm serious. No more beating ourselves up. Those ghosts made us angry when they passed through us, but I shouldn't have said the things I said to you both. I'm sorry."

"I'm sorry too. And I actually really like your style," added Mona, flicking Kit's tie up to hit them in the face.

Big, sloppy tears fell from Torpid's eyes as he brought his friends in for another hug. "And I'm sorry too. I didn't like being mean and angry."

Kit broke free first, their cheeks growing red. They cleared their throat and got up to their feet. "Good, we're all forgiven, then. We need to focus on how we're going to get out of here. That's what a team would do."

Torpid brightened. "So, we're a team again?"

Kit shrugged. "I guess I can hang with you nerds for a while longer. What do you say?" They held out their hand for Mona.

Mona took Kit's hand. "I'm in."

All on their feet again, Torpid put out his hand before them. Mona and Kit joined in and on three, they raised their hands in the air and jumped like a team of football players about to kick some serious butt. "Go, team!"

Mona felt the chain around her neck move and slip out from her T-shirt collar as she jumped. The golden glow it radiated sparkled in the dark room.

Torpid halted, his cheering coming to an abrupt stop, and stared at her. "What's that around your neck?"

"Oh, this." Mona held out the chain with the glass vial, the gold sand twinkling at her. "Sandman gave it to me back on board the Sanctuary right before Boogie arrived. He told me that it was his most cherished possession. That he trusted me to protect it."

A wide smile spread across the sloth's face and he clapped in excitement.

"Why are you so happy?" asked Mona with a raised eyebrow.

"Yeah, you do realize we've been captured, don't you?" said Kit.

Torpid bounced around the room like a spoiled kid on Christmas morning. "Don't you two see what this means?"

Mona laughed at the sloth's hopping around. Kangaroos had nothing on him. "Not following you here, Torpid."

He stopped before them and pointed at the pendant. "That's Sandman's vial."

"Yes …," said Mona, still waiting to see what all the fuss was about.

"All Dream Weavers who have mastered the sand have them," the sloth explained.

Mona rolled the vial in her fingers. "I saw Boogie destroy Raya's vial in my nightmare. He did something to the sand inside, like he sucked it up into himself. It made his eyes turn black."

Boogie had one too, back at the cottage. A crescent-moon vial.

"Yes," said Torpid. "The vials are the source of a Dream Weaver's power."

Mona's eyes widened, the dots connecting as she thought about what happened with Raya. "So, you mean …"

Torpid nodded, barely containing his excitement. "Yes."

Kit stepped between them. "Okay, will one of you please explain what's going on here?"

"Without the vial, Boogie can't take Sandman's power," said Torpid, confirming what Mona concluded.

Boogie couldn't steal Sandman's power the way he did Raya. He was missing one vital thing, and Mona had carried it with her the whole time.

Torpid fist-pumped the air. "Which also means we still have a chance of beating Boogie."

Torpid was right. If Boogie was so desperate to claim Sandman's power, he would keep the old man alive until he found the vial.

It wasn't over. Not by a long shot. "We still have a chance to make things right," Mona said, a sense of resolve running through her strong and unbreakable as titanium. "We'll get you back to your family, Kit. And Torpid, we're going to get yours back."

Mona would make it up to them. All of them. She paced the room, her mind in overdrive. "We're going to break out of here, get my sand back, find Sandman, and destroy Boogie once and for all."

Torpid looked up at her. "You really think we can do this?"

Mona smacked a fist on her palm. "I know we can."

"You're forgetting one thing," interrupted Kit, pointing a thumb to the door. "We're still locked in here."

"Oh, I'm sure we can think of something," said Mona, a grin spreading across her face. "Bedbugs might bite, but I bite back."

21

ESCAPES AND ESCAPADES

A knee dug into Mona's back. "Ouch, hurry up, will you?"

Torpid shuffled from foot to foot, staring up at the window. "I don't know if I can do this."

"You're the only one who will fit," said Kit above her, getting to their feet on Mona's back so they could make the most of their height and hoist the sloth to the open ledge.

"Torpid, you can do this. You're the bravest sloth I know."

His face lit up. "I am?"

"Yes," she said, which wasn't exactly a lie. Torpid was the only sloth she knew. "Now come on. Sandman needs you."

It was the right thing to say. Torpid set his jaw and

began his ascent up the makeshift ladder of bodies. He scurried up, his butt in Mona's face for only the briefest of moments, and Kit helped him shuffle up to the ledge.

Torpid peeked out over the edge and gulped. "It's a long way down."

"Then you better hurry up," she said, her patience wearing thin as Kit climbed off her.

"You can do it, Torpid," called Kit. "Just use the vines like you did the cobwebs in the cave."

Torpid smiled. "Hey, you've stopped calling me Weird Hairy Guy."

Kit shrugged. "Yeah, well, we're friends now, aren't we?"

"We are," said Torpid. "I'll be back before you can say pneumonoultramicroscopicsilicovolcanoconiosis."

And with that, the sloth disappeared out of sight, scaling the wall of the big mansion.

Kit blinked. "What?"

"It's the longest word in the dictionary," said Mona, wiping the dust off her clothes "A kind of lung disease you get from inhaling the dangerous air that lingers after a volcanic explosion."

"Nerds," said Kit, shaking their head. "How on earth do you know that?"

"What? I like trivia shows. It's either that or Ms. Gloomberg's soap operas back at the orphanage." Ms.

Gloomberg loved her soaps. She fell in love with every male lead. Mona even heard her call out for one of the dudes in her sleep.

"No cable, then?" asked Kit.

Mona laughed. "The only cable we have is the loose one from the ceiling that sparks sometimes."

"Well, that sounds like a safe place to keep children."

"Oh yeah," said Mona. "The Hilton has nothing on us."

"Psst."

"Pardon you," said Kit, scrunching their nose.

Mona's mouth fell open. "That wasn't me."

"Whoever denied it, supplied it," Kit said, taking a few steps away from her.

"Yeah, well, whoever smelt it, dealt it," she countered.

"Psst."

Kit waved a hand in front of their face. "There you go again."

"No, that was definitely you this time."

"This time?" said Kit. "So, it was you before."

Mona stomped her foot. "That's not what I meant."

"Psst, guys."

Mona followed the noise that turned out not to be Kit passing gas. Torpid stood behind them, swinging a key around one of his claws and leaning against the open door. "Like taking keys from a bedbug."

"Nice," said Kit, nodding their approval.

Mona high-fived her companions. "Let's get out of here."

*M*ona pinched her nose. "They stink."

Before them, a gang of bedbugs lay sprawled all over the floor, snoring into the night.

"I don't know how Boogie puts up with it." Kit waved their hand in front of their face, having something to really complain about this time. The whole foyer of the mansion smelled like a pigsty at a run-down petting zoo after dinnertime.

"Maybe he has no sense of smell as well as no conscience?" mused Mona, scanning over the sleeping bugs from the top of the stairs.

"That one," said Torpid, pointing across the foyer. "It's holding it in its pincer."

Mona groaned. "Of course it is." Her belt was tied into a loop and clutched by an orange, sleeping bug with large, crab-like claws.

Kit whistled. "He looks like he spends a lot of time at the gym."

Mona gaped at it. "He looks like he's eaten a guy

named Jim." The bug was easily the biggest of the horde, six feet of muscle and pincers that looked like they could crack coconuts with the merest clench.

Torpid wrung his hands as he peeked over the staircase. "Rock, paper, scissors on who has to go get it?"

Mona sighed. "I'll do it." It was her belt, after all, and they needed it if they were going to have the slightest chance of facing Boogie.

"We've got your back," said Kit, close behind her with Torpid in tow.

The piano still played its melancholy song that bled throughout the house, like a warped lullaby that lulled the bugs into a snore-filled slumber.

Mona winced as the floorboards creaked under her weight. It would only take one of them to wake up and alarm the others, and there were too many bugs to outrun.

Her body froze at a noise that began to rise from the left-side corridor. A noise she'd heard before.

"The ghosts," she hissed, taking the last three steps in a jump and landing with a humph.

The three of them ducked behind one of the bugs, some kind of juiced-up dung beetle, and watched as the ghosts arrived through the corridor, muttering and snapping at each other in a babble of anger.

"They're going to wake the bugs," whispered Torpid, his teeth chattering.

Torpid was right. Any moment now, the infestation of insects would rouse. Mona looked between the ghosts and the bugs. "I have an idea."

"Uh-oh," said Kit.

Mona waited as the ghosts got close enough. "Just be ready when I give the signal."

"What signal?" asked Torpid.

"This." Mona ran out from behind the dung beetle and waved her arms. "Hey, ghosts! You guys are dead. Move on already."

"Yeah, if you see a light, walk toward it," called Kit, following her lead.

"They don't have legs," cried Torpid, catching up behind them as the dung beetle stirred.

Grunts and groans grumbled around their feet as the bedbugs began to wake. They were not happy to be woken from their beauty sleep, and oh boy, did they need it.

Mona brought her fingers to her lips and whistled like a cowboy at a rodeo, ready to herd a flock of cattle.

The bugs stopped what they were doing and turned their big ugly heads to where the trio stood. The ghosts halted their arguing for a second and narrowed their haunted eyes at them, fury and outrage radiating from their hovering, misty forms.

Mona wiggled her eyebrows. "Catch us if you can."

The bugs roared. The ghosts screamed. And the three of them ran.

"Spread out," Mona called to Kit and Torpid, pointing to either side of her.

Off they went, breaking apart and running through the horde of confused bugs, sliding under legs, jumping over those still getting up, weaving through the crowd, grabbing their attention before darting off to the next bug.

It was chaos. Sweet, beautiful chaos.

The ghosts chased after Mona, Kit, and Torpid, close on their tails and colliding into and through the bugs as they went.

The bugs bounded for them, grabbing with meaty fists and releasing rumbling growls when they missed, crashing into their comrades as they tried to scramble into formation.

But they couldn't rally together and act as a regimented unit going after their three targets. Not when the effects of the ghosts passing through them started to come into play. Not when they pushed and shoved other bugs out of the way and turned on each other, swinging punches and yelling back and forth in their guttural tongue.

Mona ducked and dove her way amid the mess of monsters, searching for the one who had her belt.

It wasn't hard to find him, given that the bug stood head and shoulders over the others around him. Kit and Torpid stopped next to her and took in the sheer size of the orange bug up close.

It cocked its head and watched them like a dinosaur would an ant. It clung to the belt with one of its pincers, the bags of sand dangling from it.

"We really should've thought this one through," said Kit, craning their neck at the bug.

Mona swallowed. "Yep."

The bug took a step forward and the ground shook, sending a tremor all the way up Mona's body, from her feet to her fingertips. It snapped at them in warning with its free pincer, lowering its head and staring at them with the dark eyes of a hunter squaring up its next meal.

"We're going to have to make a run for it, aren't we?" asked Kit as the bug tossed its head back and let out a bone-rattling war cry.

"Oh yeah," said Mona.

"Run!" yelled Torpid, scampering away as the bug swung its pincer down and tried to knock them away like bowling pins.

"No!" called Kit. "We need the sand."

Mona and Kit dove to the floor just in time.

Torpid tried to run back to them, but a gaggle of ghosts swooped down from high above and shot like bullets straight for him. Mona lost sight of him in the crowd as she got to her feet.

Kit was right. They needed the sand. Without it, they would be helpless against Boogie.

"Two against one?" Kit asked her.

"I like those odds," she said, lying through her teeth. The odds were not in their favor. At all.

They shared a nod and charged at the beast-like bug from either side. It snapped at Mona, but she dodged it, giving Kit time to run up and release a kick right between its legs.

The bug let out a grunt as its eyes rolled around in its sockets, and he fell to his knees.

It was a low blow, sure, but all rules were out the window in this fight. Mona wasted no time and made the most of the temporary advantage. She sprung from the ground and jumped onto the bug's back.

The bug jerked as soon as she landed and stumbled to its feet. Mona hung on to its bulging neck as it thrashed around, trying to knock her off.

Kit flashed to her side and then was gone as the bug spun around and around trying to get her off, its pincers too big and stiff to reach back and attack her.

"Got it," came Kit's voice. Mona caught sight of the belt in Kit's hands and let go. She fell to the floor, her knee screaming upon impact as she landed hard on it with all her weight.

"Torpid, catch!" Kit aimed at the horde of livid bugs and squabbling ghosts and threw the belt.

Torpid broke out from the crowd and leaped into the air with a bounce. He caught the belt in his arms with a cheer and skidded back to the ground.

"Run!" cried Mona, waving her hand to the right-side corridor. They needed to get out of there fast.

Torpid didn't need to be told twice and headed for the corridor, the rest of the enemies too wrapped up in the pandemonium and their own paranormal rage.

Mona got up and saw the orange bug charging toward Kit, vengeance in its bulging eyes.

"Watch out!" she cried.

Kit spun on their heels but was too late. The gargantuan bug careened forward and caught Kit with its muscled arm like he was scooping up a baby.

Kit fought to get free, but it was no use. The bug had them good and squeezed anytime Kit moved.

"Kit," cried Mona, rolling up the sleeves of her hoodie as she made for Kit's captor.

Kit shook their head. "Get out of here while you still can."

The bug turned and set its sights on her, a sneer slashed across its hideous face. "No, I won't leave you."

They were a team, and no one got left behind. Not now.

The bug snorted and kicked back with its leg, sizing her up. She refused to move, refused to back down. Not when the bug had her friend.

"You're Sandman's apprentice," said Kit, their voice strained from the vise grip of the bug's bulging, muscled arm. "If anyone has a chance of defeating Boogie, it's you. Now go!"

Mona hesitated. Kit was right. Only she could use the sand. If she got captured again, then the bugs would make sure she didn't escape a second time. Sandman's life depended on her, as did the hopes and dreams of everyone he touched with his magic.

But it would mean abandoning Kit. Her heart ached, torn between doing what was necessary, and what her heart wanted.

"Go!" ordered Kit, and they reached out and punched the bug in the face. It wouldn't hurt the thing, but it was enough to break its concentration from Mona.

With one last pained look at Kit, Mona forced herself to turn and run after Torpid. Tears streamed down her face as she bolted through the corridor unfollowed and left her friend to the bugs and ghosts.

22

THE LABYRINTH OF FEAR

*M*ona found Torpid waiting at the bottom of the corridor.

"Where's Kit?" he asked.

Mona bent over, hands on knees as she caught her breath, tears running down her cheeks and dripping off her chin. "They're not coming," she said between pants, her voice catching.

"What do you mean, not coming?"

Mona swiped at her eyes. "The bugs got them."

Torpid clenched his jaw and handed over her belt. "Then we go back and get them. We have the sand now."

"No, we can't. We have to move forward." Mona fastened the belt around her waist. The sand radiated a comforting warmth, twinkling from inside their pouches, but even that couldn't cheer her right now.

"But they're our friend," exclaimed Torpid. "Kit is part of the team."

Mona brushed a hand over the pouches. She loosened the drawstring to one of them and looked back down the corridor she'd just come from.

No, she couldn't. She resealed the pouch with reluctant fingers. "I know," she said, "and Kit sacrificed themselves so we could reach Sandman. If we go back, the bugs could capture us again, and what Kit did would all be for nothing."

Torpid bowed his head. "Oh, Kit."

"I'm sorry," said Mona, willing tears not to fall. "I want to go back too, but we can't risk it."

The last image she had of Kit jabbed at her gut, of the big orange bug carrying them away. What Kit did was brave, and she refused to let that bravery be fruitless. Every part of her cried to rescue her friend, but that wasn't what Kit wanted. They did it for a reason.

"In that case, we can't let Kit down," said Torpid.

Mona straightened up and tightened her belt. It was game time, and she couldn't falter now. "You're right. We need to reach Sandman and end this once and for all."

Torpid held out his hand. Mona took it and they continued down the hall together with heavy hearts.

After a few wrong turns and a dead end or two, Mona and Kit finally found the door leading outside. They slipped outside and closed the door behind them.

Down stone steps they went and out into the back-yard. A path was laid out for them all the way down the abandoned-looking garden to the mouth of the maze Mona had seen through the window inside the mansion.

Marble statues lined the path, stone hellhounds with faces chiseled into snarls and canines bared. They were chipped and moss covered and had eyes that blinked.

Mona gripped Torpid's hand harder than necessary as they walked on.

Gravel crunched under their feet, stark white against the deep, dark green of the weeds and towering hedges that loomed over them.

They stopped at the entrance and peered beyond. Hedges lined the path straight down for a hundred yards, then they forked in two different directions leading deeper into the tangled maze.

There was nothing else inside as far as they could see. Just hedged walls and the gravel path. Yet Mona couldn't shift the unease building inside her. It was like she was a mouse, about to walk into a trap.

A booming voice filled the air in a shock of sound

amid the silence, like ferocious thunder crashing through the night sky.

"Mona, Torpid, you've finally made it," came Boogie's voice. "Though it appears you're missing someone."

"Yeah, and you're gonna pay for that one," called Mona.

She and Torpid took a step back from the mouth of the maze, turning around in search of the man, but he was nowhere and everywhere at the same time.

"Feisty, aren't you," replied his voice, like this was all some sort of amusing game they were playing.

"You have no idea," said Mona through gritted teeth.

"Well, I suppose if you're going to make me pay, then you had better come and get me."

A whirl of black burst from inside the maze and Boogie appeared in the flesh. "I have the old man with me."

Mona lunged forward, but Torpid got in front of her and held her back. "Mona, what if he wants us to go in there? What if it's part of some plan?"

"It definitely is," said Mona, eyes fixed on her enemy. "But there's no other way, and Sandman is somewhere inside."

The podium from her nightmare lay in the center,

and Mona would bet everything that Boogie held Sandman there.

Boogie motioned with a wave of his arm for them to enter, like a pleasant doorman to some swanky hotel. "Come on, step through. I'll even add in a bonus prize."

Boogie snapped his fingers and a second whirl of black sand swooshed beside him. The darkness dissipated to reveal a familiar face.

Mona gasped. "Kit."

"Yes," said Boogie, his meaty hand wrapped around Kit's neck, longs nails digging into her friend's skin. "Now, enter my Labyrinth of Fear. If you dare."

As angry as she was, every nerve in Mona's body trembled at the presence of the Boogie Man, his darkness radiating from him and sending fear through anything it touched.

Boogie yanked Kit toward him and before Mona could react, they vanished in a cloud of black. Boogie's laugh echoed from somewhere inside, taunting and evil.

Torpid waved his fist in the air. "Oh, we'll show you, Boogie, you big meanie."

And with that, Mona and Torpid entered the lion's den.

"We need to reach the center," Mona said, both of them moving at a jog.

A dense fog lingered around their feet as they delved farther into the labyrinth. It grew thicker and after a couple of turns, it misted well above their heads.

"I don't like this," said Torpid, somewhere next to her.

"Here, take my hand. It will be all right."

But Torpid's hand never came.

"Mona!" he cried, somewhere behind her.

Mona spun on her heels and headed back the way she'd come. "Torpid!"

She collided into something with a thud and toppled to the ground, gravel scuffing her palms as she broke her fall. Mona scurried back to her feet and reached out before her.

"Torpid, where are you?"

Her fingers met bristles. A hedge.

She ran her scraped hands along, panicking now. She called his name again, but there was nothing. Nothing but the wall that wasn't there just moments ago.

The walls had moved. The maze was alive.

*M*ona ran forward, calling out for her lost friend. Maybe if she rounded in a square, she could reach Torpid from the other side.

It wasn't concrete, but it was the only thing she had, and Mona held to the idea like a lifeline as she quickened to a run and traveled through the maze.

She spun around a corner and sprinted down a long, straight section of the pathway, calling out for Torpid like a mantra. Like she could make him appear if she just wished it enough.

A rushing sound erupted from somewhere ahead, the ground vibrating with a low rumble. Mona stopped where she was and listened as it grew louder and louder.

Her heart drummed in her ears, a cramp clawing at her side.

Something was coming.

Right then, a tidal wave of black sand came rushing around the corner and headed straight for her, crashing against the hedged walls of the labyrinth.

Mona ran, but the sand was too fast. It swept her up and off her feet, wrapping her in darkness.

It was like one of her nightmares. The sand circled around her, the force ringing in her ears and whipping her hair and clothes.

Then, as quickly as it had hit her, the sand stopped.

Mona blinked grit out of her eyes and inhaled a shocked breath. She was back at Ms. Gloomberg's Home for Wayward Children.

She didn't know how, or why, but she was there. Like she had never left.

The crayon stars stared down at her from the ceiling as she lay in her old bed with the sheets over her shoulders. Mona sat up slowly and looked around the bedroom.

Ally wasn't in her bed.

Mona kicked off the covers and got up, taking hesitant steps toward the door. The hallway was deserted, the lack of noise from the other kids giving the place an eerie feel.

Mona crossed the hall and shoved open the door nearest the stairs. She ducked her head inside and frowned. George wasn't in his room either. None of the other kids were there.

"Ms. Gloomberg?" she called, going downstairs. The floorboards creaked with every step.

Reaching the bottom of the stairs, Mona went to the director's office and knocked on the door. "Ms. Gloomberg?"

No one answered, the old woman's usual croak telling her to go away missing. Mona turned the handle and went inside. The room was empty, just like everywhere else in the home.

She was alone.

Mona took a seat across from Ms. Gloomberg's desk, a place she had sat so many times before, receiving lecture after lecture about how much trouble she was. She sat in silence, like if she waited there long enough, the old woman would come in and reprimand her for something she was most likely guilty of. She would deny it, of course.

Yet the director didn't show. No one did.

Mona lost track of how long she sat there, hands clasped. Loneliness seeped in through her skin and down to the bone, making her hollow. Where was everyone? Had they all gone somewhere without her? Did they not want her around anymore?

Had they all been adopted, every one of them now with loving families to call their own? All except her. No one wanted her. No one had ever wanted her.

Mona curled up on the chair, hugging her legs close to her chest. She was alone in the world. She had no one.

A voice whispered through the window, faint, almost as if her own thoughts were speaking to her. "No family. No friends. What do you have left?" asked the deep voice.

Wait. That voice. She knew that voice. She'd heard it before.

But where?

Then it hit her. It hit her harder than the third grade kid had on her first day of school.

Boogie.

It all came rushing back to her. Sandman. The Land of Nightmares. The maze.

Kit. Torpid.

She looked around. None of it was real. It was a nightmare. Something Boogie made up to make her lose herself.

He would have to try harder than that. She had a job to do, people to save, and things to make up for, and she wasn't about to let some nightmare stop her. Not by a long shot.

The voice repeated itself, louder this time, and most definitely Boogie's. "No family. No friends. What do you have left?"

Mona sat up in the chair and raised her head. "Myself."

The voice sniggered. "Yourself?"

"Yes, myself. No matter what happens, I will always have myself." She stood from the chair, kicking it back to the floor. "This is a dream. It's not real."

A roar of frustration boomed inside the office.

A great sucking sound filled the room, like a vacuum on hyper power. The orphanage began to break apart. Cracks split down the walls, plaster dropping from the ceiling and bursting into dust. Chairs and tables flew past her face and crumbled before her eyes. The house shook as the pressure grew, the contents of the home flying around and around, until the pressure got to be too much.

With a bang, the image before Mona burst. Blasts of black sand filled the air as the orphanage and everything in it exploded into nothing but sand.

Mona swatted the air before her, swiping away the sand. She was back in the maze.

No, she had never left. It was all an illusion. A trick of Boogie's.

Fake.

"Nice try," she said, hoping he could hear her.

She gathered herself and set off again, faster and with more purpose.

She hadn't gotten very far when a voice cried through the fog. A different one this time.

"No!" someone screamed.

Mona followed the cries, turning left, then right, and running down a path until she came across a dead end.

"No, please. I'm here. Can't you see me?"

"Kit!" she called, stopping a few feet from them.

Black sand circled around Kit, trapping them in a vortex of darkness they couldn't escape.

Mona called for them again, but Kit couldn't hear her.

Mona backed up to give herself some space and then ran. She charged for the tornado of sand and jumped right into the eye of the storm.

Just like before, the sand encompassed her. It swooped and spun and spiraled in a blast of energy, growing in intensity until it stopped in an abrupt flash.

Mona blinked and this time she was standing outside a house. Roses grew in pots under the windows, the garden neatly tended and surrounded by a white picket fence.

A woman in her late thirties was taking down a sign pitched in the mowed lawn, her face grim and pinched in at the cheeks. She had dark hair and skin as pale as milk.

A tall man with cropped brown hair and glasses walked up to her and took the sign. He moved like a dazed zombie to the open garage and tossed the sign inside, not bothering to close the metal door as he walked back toward the house.

Mona leaned over the fence and caught a glimpse of the image on the sign. It was Kit's face, framed with the words "Missing" and "Have you seen our child?"

"Mom, Dad. It's me, Kit."

Mona turned to see Kit, running through the gate and over the lawn to reach their mom.

"I've come back," said Kit, desperation in every word.

The woman didn't react. She looked straight through Kit like they weren't there.

Mona watched from the fence, wincing at Kit's pain. Their mother seemed to be devoid of emotion, like a hollow shell of a human who had no more emotion left to give.

Kit tried to reach out to her, but no matter how far they reached, something held them back, never quite being able to meet their mom. They gave up and tried their dad, but again, he didn't appear to notice Kit's presence.

Mona walked up to them like she was approaching a frightened stray cat.

"They can't see me," said Kit when Mona reached out and squeezed their shoulder. "They've given up on ever finding me."

"No, they haven't," she said.

Kit shook their head, panic in their eyes, wide and bright with fear like headlights in the night. "They must think I ran away. That I was unhappy. What if my parents think this is their fault?" Kit paced up and down the garden path.

Mona let them lap around twice before getting in their way. "Kit, you need to snap out of it. None of this is real."

"It is. Look." Kit's parents stared out into the lawn where the sign once stood, before they turned and entered the house, closing the door shut behind them.

Kit dropped to their knees, tears streaming freely down their crumpled face. "Mom! Dad! Please."

Mona grabbed the back of Kit's shirt. "Get up."

Kit shook their head and stared at the ground. "There's no point."

"Yes, there is," said Mona, her voice sharp and forceful. She had to make Kit see, to snap them out of their grief long enough to see it all for what it was. "Your family is waiting for you to come home, and you can't just sit here."

"Mona?" said Kit, as if seeing her for the first time. "What are you doing here?"

Mona allowed a gentle smile before she scooped her arms under Kit's. "I'm saving your butt, again."

"What are you doing?" asked Kit, worming under her grip.

"Up. Now," she ordered, pulling them up with all her strength.

"Wait," said Kit, once they were back on their feet. "How did you get here?"

"How did *you* get here?" she asked.

Kit scratched their head. "I don't know."

"Think about it."

"The bugs dragged me off to Boogie. And then …" Kit's eyes lit up as realization kicked in.

Mona nodded. "See? All a dream."

Kit took some time to gather themselves, eyeing the scene with a scrutinizing stare. "It is," they said eventually. "This is just one of Boogie's nightmares."

And with the sudden realization came the breakdown of Boogie's illusion. The house began to fall apart, first the tiles on the roof, then the bricks on the four outer walls. The picket fence flew in the air and circled around them, dancing in the sky with rose petals ripped from the heads of the neatly tended flowerpots.

The nightmare erupted and blasted away, tearing apart the illusion and bringing them back to the labyrinth.

"You okay?" asked Mona.

Kit nodded, lips set in a firm line of determination.

"Good. Now come on," said Mona. "We need to find Torpid."

---

*A*ll Mona and Kit had to do was follow the wails.

They echoed off the walls and led them deeper, right into the heart of the labyrinth. They grew louder the farther they ran, getting closer and closer with each turn.

They found Torpid trapped inside a cocoon of rushing sand like the ones she and Kit had broken out of.

"Don't stop," said Mona, grabbing Kit's hand. "Just jump."

Kit did what she said without comment and they dove into Torpid's nightmare.

"Where are we?" asked Kit once the sand calmed down.

"I don't know," said Mona. Waves rushed at their feet, soaking their shoes. A pebbled beach stretched out before them, surrounded by jagged rocks, and salt air filled her lungs. "Wait, is that what I think it is?"

They both ran toward the wreckage, upheaving sand as they went.

"Oh no," breathed Mona.

The Sanctuary lay broken and derelict in the middle of the crag of rocks, waves crashing against it and sending bits of debris and wood from the ship out to sea.

Kit nudged her. "It's a dream, remember."

Mona closed her eyes. Thank goodness.

They waded into the waves and reached the ship. The bottom of the rope ladder flapped around in the water and they used it to climb up and pull themselves on board.

Torpid was in the middle of the top deck, his wails traveling in the wind.

Mona and Kit raced over and kneeled next to him.

"Everyone's hopes and dreams," said Torpid meekly, shaking his head in sorrow. "They're lost."

Mona rubbed his arm. "No, they're not." He was so cold.

"Sandman is gone," he said, staring out into the crashing waves, the wreckage of the ship all around them. The masts had fallen and snapped in the middle, the bow completely shattered, like it had crash-landed nose first from the clouds.

"He isn't gone," Kit assured, but it fell on deaf ears.

"Boogie won," cried Torpid. "It's over."

Mona gave Torpid a shake. "He sure as heck hasn't won. We're not going to let that happen."

Torpid dropped to the floor and sobbed into the night, his shoulders heaving.

"Come on, Torpid," said Mona, resting a hand on his back. "We're a team. We're going to beat Boogie together."

"A team," said the sloth, sitting up with a jolt.

"Yes," said Mona. "We haven't defeated Boogie yet, and Sandman is waiting for us to save him, remember?"

Kit bent down and got the sloth to his feet. "This is

a dream, Torpid. You know a dream when you see one. Look around."

Torpid did. "It is a dream. Oh, that Boogie is a terrible, terrible person for making me believe this."

Mona held out her hand before them all. Kit caught on and placed their hand on top of hers. "Come on, Torpid. What do you say?"

A smile spread across the sloth's face. He placed his hand at the top of the pile and as one, they threw their hands into the air and yelled, "Go, team!"

And, like that, the nightmare evaporated into sand, returning them to the maze and to the task they had journeyed so far to complete. It was time to end this once and for all.

As a team, Mona, Kit, and Torpid took a final turn, the dome of the podium in sight over the hedged wall, and entered the center of their enemy's Labyrinth of Fear.

Boogie stood at the top of the podium, waiting. And he had his whole entire army of bedbugs with him.

23

THE BATTLE OF THE SANDS

*A*s far as welcome parties went, this one was packed.

Mona looked out over the field surrounding the podium, every inch of it filled with bedbugs, each one uglier than the hideous monster next to it.

The bugs snarled and taunted the trio with monstrous grunts, teeth bared, tails whipping, pincers snapping, and knuckles cracking. They moved from side to side, shifting their weight, eyes hungry, just waiting for the order to strike.

A flash of lightning split the sky in half in a spark of white, ripping it open. Rain hurtled down as thunder boomed so loud it made Mona's ears ring.

The rain had them soaked in seconds, falling so

hard it bounced up from the ground after the drops landed, soaking them further.

The lightning flashed again, and Mona caught a better look at the podium.

Mona straightened. "Sandman."

Sandman was tied around one of the spiraling pillars of the podium, the bindings tight around his weak frame. His once-pristine clothes were dirty and ragged, seeming baggier on him than they had been. His head lolled on his chest, hat missing, the rope the only thing keeping him from falling to the stone floor.

Torpid suppressed a whimper. "Is he—"

"I don't know," said Mona, turning her attention to the one responsible.

Boogie stood in front of the pillar holding Sandman, his black eyes alight from the lightning. Energy crackled in the air, his presence domineering and magic palpable even from where Mona stood.

"I'm going to show you what a real nightmare is," she vowed, running her hand over the pouches of sand. They answered to her touch, twinkling at her as a rush of warmth surged up from her fingertips. The sand was ready to fight with her.

Boogie sniggered, his voice booming like before, as if he were connected to a set of massive speakers. "Don't go making threats you can't keep, kid."

"Oh, it's not a threat," Mona replied. "It's a promise."

"Well, come on up and show me what you've got." Boogie gestured down past the stone steps of the podium and across the field of bugs. "If you can make it past my friends, of course."

"Coward," spat Mona. He was hiding behind his horde instead of facing her head-on. Typical bully. But bullies had a habit of underestimating her, and she was going to show Boogie just how wrong that was.

The enemies stood waiting, Mona, Kit, and Torpid at one side, the bugs and Boogie at the other. The rain continued to fall as a silence settled over the field.

"I need to get to Boogie," murmured Mona to her friends, never letting her eyes leave her target as he stood above them with an amused face, like a spectator about to watch a show.

"Don't worry," said Torpid, "we'll clear your path."

"And how exactly do you expect us to do that?" replied Kit, nodding to the sheer number and size of the bedbug horde. They were outweighed, outnumbered, out-powered, and out-uglied.

"I know," said Mona, opening her pouches. It felt so good to have them by her side again. Jolts of warmth spread over her as she dug inside the bags, feeling more than choosing which colors to use.

She took a handful of the orange sand and mixed

it with red and yellow. Closing her eyes, Mona returned herself to the nightmare she had of Boogie losing Katherine. Of the cribs the children would never sleep in.

Picturing the carved creature on the first crib, Mona tossed the sand in the air, focused.

"Wow," said Kit, and Mona opened her eyes.

A ball of fire floated in the air in front of her and warmed her face. It grew, getting bigger and bigger until a valiant cry broke from the flames. Something shot out of the ball of fire and flew through the sky.

Mona awed at the magnificent bird as it flapped its long wings and circled above them. Even the bedbugs watched. Tendrils of flames emitted from its feathered tail, leaving a trail like sparklers on the Fourth of July.

The phoenix flew down to the ground and bowed its head to Mona. Its flame-colored feathers sparkled, not fully formed the way they should be, but it lit up the night like a beacon.

"Torpid, hop on."

The phoenix turned to the sloth and lowered its feathers to allow him to ride.

Torpid looked from the phoenix to Mona. "Me?"

"Yes. Attack them from the sky." Mona patted the phoenix on the head, and it cooed. "She'll know what to do."

Torpid swallowed and then wriggled on to the back

of the bird. It let out another brilliant cry and then took off, Torpid yelping the whole way.

Mona was already moving on to her next conjure.

Taking out piles of pink and purple, Mona visualized the second crib and the image Boogie had carved into it.

With a wave of her hand, Mona asked the sand to compile into what she wanted, and by the time she opened her eyes, the unicorn was standing next to her, awaiting instructions.

Mona gaped, looking at her hands. It wasn't a perfect unicorn by any means. It was larger, more like one of those beasts the cops rode on in the city park, and its horn was a little off-kilter, but it was magnificent.

The sand had settled into the real textures of what she conjured this time, the pink body of the unicorn decorated with long locks of purple hair on its mane and tail.

Kit glowered at Mona. "Really?"

The unicorn neighed and rubbed its head up against Kit's arm. It looked like something straight out of a fairy tale.

Mona giggled. "Aw, I think it suits you. Besides, that horn should do some damage. Just tell it where to go."

Kit groaned, but Mona caught them staring in

wonder as they climbed on. "Does it fart rainbows too?" Kit asked once they were sitting on the creature's back.

"I sincerely hope so." Mona slapped the unicorn on its rump. It reared up on its hind legs with a beautiful yet don't-mess-with-me war cry and charge forward into the fray of bedbugs.

The phoenix took that as a sign and it darted from the sky like an arrow. It swooped down, reaching out with its talons, and grabbed one of the bedbugs on the front line. The phoenix swirled in the air and let go of the bug, launching it smack into the horde and knocking them to the ground in a pile of confusion.

Torpid cheered into the night as the phoenix rose again to aim another attack.

Mona darted behind Kit and their unicorn as it created a pathway through the army. She ducked and leaped over the bugs who dared get in the magnificent creature's way. The bugs yelped as they were tossed aside and squirmed on the ground as the unicorn trampled over the creatures with a *crunch*.

Kit and Torpid led their creatures in the onslaught, pulverizing any bug that got in their way. Mona reached the bottom of the stairs leading up to the podium in a matter of minutes.

The orange bug from before stepped out from the battlefield and blocked Mona's way, roaring into her face. It snapped at her with a clawed pincer and Mona dove to the ground. She rummaged in a pouch as she got to her feet, just as the bug sent another attack her way.

It caught her in the side and sent her careening back. She landed with a hard smack.

Mona gasped for air, the blow winding her and making her lungs burn.

The orange bug stood over her and let out a deep, satisfied laugh. Mona tried to get to her feet, but the bug shoved her back down with a lazy foot.

She fumbled with her belt, her eyes watering as she gasped for air.

The bug drew a muscled arm back, ready to swing and snap at her.

Mona rolled, narrowly missing the pincer.

Her attacker tried again, but this time she was ready for him. Mona lunged as the sand she held solidified into a baseball bat. She swung it as hard as she could.

The bat cracked the bug's head with a clang. The bug blinked a few times before its eyes rolled to the back of its head and it fell, out cold.

Mona nudged the giant bug with the tip of the bat and declared, "Strike! You're out," punching the air in triumph.

She moved her attention to the podium.

Boogie was at Sandman now, holding the old man's face with his long-nailed hands. Boogie whispered into Sandman's ear, sneering as electricity crackled from him. Sandman's eyes flew open and he winced in pain as his face turned gray.

Mona had to do something. Fast.

"Hey, Boogie," she called. "I think I have something you might be looking for." Mona dug out the chain from inside her T-shirt and flashed Sandman's vial of power at him.

Boogie didn't say a word. He let go of Sandman and turned to face her. His features darkened and he threw out his arms in her direction. Black sand flew from the piles around him and headed straight for her like snakes.

No, not *like* snakes. They *were* snakes.

Mona aimed her bat at the forms of conjured sand, but it did little to stop their attack. The snakes hissed and wrapped themselves around her, coiling in a tight, immobilizing squeeze.

The bat fell from her hand. Boogie waved again with his arms and the snakes returned to him, taking their bounty with them.

They stopped in front of Boogie and dropped Mona to the floor before evaporating back into sand.

"So nice of you to join me, Mona," said Boogie, reaching for her. "Now hand over that vial."

24
THE FINAL DREAM

*M*ona reacted on pure instinct.

Boogie's black fingernails reached to grab her neck. Digging her hand into the nearest pouch on her belt, she threw a fist of sand in his face.

Boogie winced, closed his eyes, and stepped back, swiping at his face.

Mona wasted no time. She got up and ran to Sandman, still tied to the pillar.

"Sandman, wake up." Mona raised his head and tapped on the side of his face.

Sandman's eyes pried open, lids heavy with fatigue.

"Wake up," she said. "We have to get you out of here."

Sandman stared at her for a moment until comprehension kicked him into gear. Fear grew in his eyes. "Run, Mona. Get you and your friends out of here."

"No. I'm not leaving you behind. It's my fault you're here." Mona yanked at the ropes binding the old man to the stone pillar, but there was no knot. It was held together by magic and no matter how much she tugged, it wouldn't release its prisoner.

"The fault lies with the man who brought me here," began Sandman, but Boogie came from behind and threw some of his black sand at Sandman, hitting him directly in the face. Sandman slumped forward against the ropes, unmoving and face slack.

Mona darted behind the pillar, anything to put some distance between her and the master of nightmares.

"You're not going anywhere," said Boogie, walking around the pillar. "Not until you give me that vial."

"Never," said Mona, circling the pillar in time with Boogie as her mind fought to think of a plan.

Taking more fistfuls of sand, Mona tossed it in the air and tried to concentrate. Shapes began to form, but before they could solidify, Boogie lashed out with his own sand and smothered her conjure into smithereens.

A cry came from the field. The phoenix was falling through the sky, Torpid still on her back. The bugs were throwing things at them and something sharp struck true. The phoenix plunged to the ground and burst into fire-colored sand upon impact.

"Torpid!" she cried, but the bugs surrounded the crash-landing of the phoenix and blocked any sight of the brave little sloth.

Mona forced her eyes back to Boogie, her hands working on a new conjure as she hurried along the perimeter of the podium, weaving between the other pillars to block Boogie's attacks.

He sent snake after snake at her, each of them hitting off the stone and smashing back to black grains.

Mona pressed her back against a pillar and stilled, listening for any sign of Boogie's location. His laughter echoed around the domed podium, sending icicles down her spine.

There was more commotion going on in the field. A cheer resounded from the bugs and Mona risked a glance.

Kit and their unicorn were galloping through the bugs, heading toward the spot where the phoenix had fallen. Kit's cries carried on the wind as the unicorn, head down and horn out, raced through their enemies like they were nothing.

But they never saw the attack coming. A gang of bugs came from the rear and sprang on them. The unicorn lost her balance and tripped, sending Kit flying. The bug in charge bounded on top of the unicorn like a lion catching its prey. The bugs piled on to each other, adding weight to the mound until a burst of pink and purple sand erupted from under them.

"You don't have to do this," Mona called to Boogie. Her friends were in danger.

"I want to, and I will," came his voice.

It was right behind her.

Mona slid down the pillar to the floor, just missing Boogie's arms wrapping around the stone above. He roared in frustration.

"You're going to destroy hope for everyone," she shouted, crawling across the ground. "Take away their dreams."

"Yes, that's the plan." His footsteps followed her, slow and deliberate.

"Why? Why are you doing this?" Mona scooped up yellow sand in her hand and thrust it out behind her. An explosion of sunlight burst into the podium, bright and brilliant.

Mona ran across the podium as Boogie grimaced at the light. "Because hopes and dreams are evil!" he yelled, his sand swooping up to the ball of light, smothering it into darkness.

"Evil?" called Mona, moving again.

Boogie launched a tirade of sand at the spot where Mona spoke from. "When I met my wife, I thought all my dreams were coming true. But they were lies, and my dream was ripped away from me."

Mona slipped out of the podium and ran across the steps, back the way she'd come. She reclaimed her dropped baseball bat and crept back inside on tiptoes.

"Dreams are cruel and unfair," Boogie said, incensed. "They bring people nothing but pain and disappointment when they don't come true."

"Oh, and fear and nightmares don't do that?" she asked, sneaking up on him. Boogie turned to her voice and Mona swung the bat for his head.

"Dreams need to be removed," Boogie said, grabbing the bat inches from his head and shoving it back, sending Mona skidding across the floor. Her back smashed against a pillar and she collapsed to the ground.

"False hopes are worse than any nightmare I could conjure," said Boogie, coming toward her.

Mona's head swam, her vision dizzy. "Hopes and dreams keep people going," she yelled, pushing herself to a sitting position. "They help them through their darkest times. They're important, even if they don't come true. Without them, people would have nothing."

Boogie cut the air with a slash of his arm. "You know nothing, girl. All of that is a lie."

Mona shook her head. "It's the truth. You've lost

sight of that. What do you think Katherine would say if she could see you now?"

"Don't you dare say her name," spat Boogie, his whole body shaking with rage.

Mona tried to get up, but her arms betrayed her. She had no energy left. "Do you think she would want you to instill fear into everyone?" she asked, trying anything to get through to him. "Was that the kind of man she married?"

Boogie grabbed her by the collar and hoisted her off the ground. "The man she married is dead. He died long ago."

Spittle hit Mona's face. Boogie was right. The man she'd seen in that dream wasn't there anymore. He'd been irreversibly altered. Overcome by grief and anger that had only festered in the years since the tragedy.

He had turned on his fellow Dream Weavers, his own friends, to stop people from dreaming, to try to stop them from experiencing a heartache like he had. But the power had consumed him, turning him into a monster. It was too late for Boogie. He was too far gone now, and nothing Mona could say or do could bring him back from the darkness.

Then it came to her, like a dream in the night.

Mona knew Boogie's dream. The thing he wanted more than anything. She knew it because it was the same dream she had, the one she would never admit to even herself—until now.

She wanted a family.

And Boogie, more than anything else in the world, the part deep down inside of his cold, black heart, wanted his family back.

It was so clear, even as she stared into the pits of his onyx eyes.

Boogie held her before him, panting from sheer anger at the hand life had dealt him and the ones he loved. He reached for the vial, the one that matched the black-filled one he carried around his own neck.

Mona slipped her fingers into a pouch on her belt and dropped a fist of sand into the air below her. She closed her eyes and charged all the remaining energy she had left into her conjuring.

Three shapes appeared behind them, three shapes that morphed and changed into people. One big, and two small.

Boogie's eyes widened. He dropped Mona and walked away from her, entranced at the sight of something he had lost. Of his dream.

Her conjure was crudely done. The largest of the three looked nothing like Katherine, and the other two never got to grow up to be the toddlers depicted before Boogie.

They were mannequin shapes really, but they were

enough. Boogie's mind did the rest, seeing what he wanted.

Two little girls ran around their mother, chasing each other, their innocent laughter ringing through the podium like a song.

Katherine sat on a chair between them, knitting and smiling at her husband.

Boogie fell to his knees before his family and they crowded around them. The children smothered him with hugs and Katherine kissed him on the cheek, her smile full of love and happiness.

Mona whispered in Boogie's ear. "Go to them," she said, tears falling down her face. "Go to your family."

Mona reached out and tugged at the vial around Boogie's neck. The chain came loose with ease.

She let it fall through her fingers to the floor and stamped down on it with her shoe, smashing the glass with a crunch.

And, just like Raya in the desert, Boogie slowly transformed into grains of sand. It covered his whole body, and yet he didn't even notice, too busy with his wife and daughters. His family.

A warm, contented smile spread across his face, and then the Boogie Man crumbled into a million glittering black granules.

25

THE AFTERMATH

Boogie's remains swept by Mona's feet in the wind.

Mona crossed the podium and reached Sandman. His bindings broke and crumpled away, and she jumped forward just in time to break the old man's fall.

"Sandman?" she asked. His skin was cold to the touch, face deathly pale.

"No," she said, panic jolting her nerves like an electric shock. "Not now."

She shook Sandman, his body limp in her arms. "Please don't go."

Mona shook him harder this time, willing him to open his eyes, to say something. Anything.

"But we did it," she said, her bottom lip shaking. "We found you and defeated Boogie. Please wake up."

Sandman didn't respond. Mona stared out at the field through blurred eyes, her tears hot as they trickled down her grimy face.

The bedbugs had stopped fighting and all of them just stood unmoving, like grotesque stone statues. Then, in a sudden eruption, they exploded, one by one, into bursts of black sand. Mona watched as the explosions ignited over the field like an intricate fireworks display.

In the distance, cheers rang, and as the storm began to fade and the sand settled, she saw Kit and Torpid hugging each other, hollering with glee.

Mona closed her eyes, her emotions a jumbled mess as she kneeled by Sandman's side. Her friends were safe. They had made it through the battle.

But perhaps not all.

Footsteps echoed through the podium as Kit and Torpid ran to meet her, giving each other a high five when they reached the top of the steps. Their faces fell at the sight of Mona.

Torpid ran to Sandman's side. "Oh dear. Sandman, are you okay?" He looked up to Mona. "What happened?"

The sloth had a bruised eye, already swelling up. Some of his fur was missing from his arm too.

"I don't know," Mona said, teardrops falling onto Sandman's unmoving body.

"Where's Boogie?" Kit asked. A smear of blood tracked from their nose, their red tie gone and shirt ripped along one side.

"Gone," said Mona. "He's with his family now."

Kit lay a hand against Mona's back, and a sob escaped her lips. Torpid lay over Sandman's chest. "Come back to us, Sandman. Come back."

A snap sounded next to them and a crack appeared the whole way up the podium Sandman had been tied to. The snapping continued as the rest of the pillars did the same, bits of rubble falling from where the cracks split the stone.

Above them, the huge dome whined, and the cracks spindled their way from the pillars up to the center of the dome.

"We have to get out of here," warned Kit as bits of stone fell from the ceiling.

"No," said Mona, leaning over Sandman to protect him from the debris. "We can't leave him."

"Mona, this place is going to cave in. We need to leave." Kit tried to pull her to her feet, but she swiped them away and turned back to Sandman.

Mona took the pendant from around her neck, the glass vial glowing with its golden sand. "I kept this safe for you. Just like you asked."

Gently raising Sandman's head, she placed the

chain over it and around his neck, returning the vial to its rightful place.

Kit picked up Torpid from the floor and carried him in their arms, the sloth lost in his grief. "Mona, get up."

Cracks had appeared on the floor now, the whole podium shaking like it was in the heart of an earthquake.

Mona took one final look at the man who'd saved her from her life at the orphanage. The man who was the first person ever to believe in her. She squeezed his hand, then tore her gaze from him and got up.

"The maze is falling apart too," said Kit, standing at the foot of the stairs.

The hedged walls of the labyrinth were turning to sand, just like the bedbugs. The sand floated in the air and circled in a black vortex that covered the sky. Mona tilted her head and saw sand breaking from the domed podium roof, adding to the mix above. "There's nowhere to go," she said, as the wind picked up speed, blowing her hair in her face.

A bright, golden glow filled the inside of the podium, glittering out into the darkness of the broken world crumbling before them.

The trio spun around, shielding their eyes from the abrupt shock of light.

"Ah," sighed Sandman, clutching his vial. "Just what I needed. A nice pick-me-up."

"Sandman!" Mona cried. She sped to him and wrapped her arms around him, Torpid leaping up into his arms.

"We thought you were gone," she said, pulling back to take him in. His cheeks were blushed pink, skin back to its usual shade, eyes bright and very much alive.

Sandman chuckled. "I'm pleased to say you were mistaken. Just very tired is all."

Torpid planted a big wet kiss on Sandman's forehead, and Sandman hugged the sloth to his chest. "Nice to see you, my friend."

Torpid cried happy tears into Sandman's arms.

"Oh, well," said Sandman, looking out into the chaos. "This is a bit of a pickle, isn't it?"

"What's happening?" asked Kit, the wind at hurricane level now, the field ripping up from the ground and flying into the vortex that sucked everything and anything up in its wide, gaping mouth, like a black hole.

"The Land of Nightmares can't exist without its creator," said Sandman, placing a protective arm in front of them all.

"It's vanishing?" asked Torpid, standing next to Mona now.

"Precisely. Not to worry though." Sandman rolled

up his sleeves. "Mona, my dear, could you pass me some of your sand? A good pinch of each color should do the trick."

Mona handed over the sand.

Sandman then threw it into the air. With a swoop of his hands, it collectivized and spread in a wide circle, growing with a brilliant white light until it was the shape and size of a large doorway.

Sandman clapped his hands, and the sand solidified into a wooden door with a simple copper knob. He opened it and waved them over. "Let's get going, shall we? I could devour a nice cup of tea and some cake."

Mona laughed, her body tired yet spirits high. The three of them followed Sandman, hand in hand, and stepped through the portal doorway, leaving the Land of Nightmares for good.

---

*M*ona stepped out of the doorway and into the light. It hurt her eyes, too used to the darkness of the nightmarish land they'd just left.

"This isn't the Sanctuary," said Torpid, looking around. "Where are we?"

"You'll see," assured Sandman, walking down the

quiet street. "We have an important task to complete before going home."

The sun was rising, shades of pink and orange reaching out over the horizon. The street seemed vaguely familiar to Mona, though she couldn't quite put her finger on why.

It was a far cry from the orphanage in the city. This was a picturesque suburban street, filled with matching houses that, in winter, would make brilliant images on Christmas cards. It was the kind of image Mona once held in her mind when she hoped to be adopted. Big gardens filled with flowers in every color, two-story houses with red-tiled roofs and white picket fences.

Kit cleared their throat as they walked along the sidewalk at a slow, relaxed pace. "About me not telling you Boogie's plans, Mr. Sandman," they began, but Sandman held a hand up.

"You don't need to explain. You had your reasons, and very good reasons they were too. You did what you had to do for your family, and no one can take offense to that." He stopped walking and rested a hand on Kit's shoulder. "And I am sorry too. I shouldn't have put you in the lower deck."

Kit shrugged. "You thought I was working for the enemy. I guess that seems fair to me. I mean, I'd do the same."

"Nevertheless," said Sandman, "it was wrong of me, and I sincerely apologize."

"Thank you, sir," said Kit, their demeanor bright and a spring in their step as they continued on. Mona watched them, noting how Kit seemed lighter, like the dark shadow they carried had been wiped away, disintegrated into nothing along with the Land of Nightmares.

"Now, speaking of family," said Sandman, waving a hand to the end of the street.

Kit stopped dead, eyes alight. "Mom. Dad."

Then it clicked. Mona had been there before, kind of. This was the street from Kit's nightmare in the labyrinth.

Kit's parents were walking out the front door, piles of paper in their hands, flyers with Kit's face on them. They hadn't forgotten about Kit. Boogie's nightmare had been a lie, and Kit's parents would never give up hope that their child would return to them one day.

"Will I see you guys again?" asked Kit, turning back to Mona, Torpid, and Sandman.

"In your dreams," jibed Mona, unable to contain her smile.

"You can come on board the Sanctuary and visit any time you wish," said Sandman.

"How will you know when I want to visit?" asked Kit.

Sandman tapped his temple. "I'll know."

Mona stepped forward and gave Kit a hug. "Go see your parents," she said, pushing them forward with a playful shove.

Kit nodded, and set off down the street, calling for their parents.

Their parents turned to Kit's voice. They dropped the flyers on the ground, the paper dancing off down the street in the morning wind, and hurried to meet Kit.

Kit's dad swept them off their feet and pulled them in for a tight embrace, their Mom joining in.

Mona, Sandman, and Torpid watched at a distance. There were a lot of tears and laughter.

"I left the ship." Torpid beamed up at Sandman.

Sandman leaned down to the sloth's level. "And for that, I am both eternally grateful and extremely proud. Perhaps now we can make a habit of leaving the Sanctuary together?"

"Oh yes, I think I'd like that." Torpid turned to Mona. "Mona, are you all right?"

Mona bowed her head, unable to meet their eyes. "I'm sorry," she said. "For everything."

Sandman sighed. "People make mistakes. Humans are very good at making them. It's how we learn. What's most important is how we react to them. You set off to right your wrongs, and in the process managed to stop one of the most powerful men in the world."

Mona stole a look at him. "Don't you hate me? I could have messed up everything."

"I could never hate you. And look how things turned out. Boogie Man is no more, you have returned Kit to their family, you saved me from losing my powers, and the hopes and dreams of everyone are finally safe again." Sandman wrapped an arm around her shoulder. "And from what I saw, your sand abilities have proved to be remarkably innate."

"I guess," she said, heat rising in her cheeks.

"I told you I believed in you," said Sandman. "Maybe now you'll believe in yourself."

And she did.

They watched Kit and their parents for a bit longer.

"A family reunited," said Sandman. "Their dreams have been answered today."

"Must be nice," said Mona. A pang of pain struck her heart as she watched Kit and their parents go into their house. She was over the moon for Kit, but it still hurt, like every time one of the kids in the orphanage said their final goodbyes when they got adopted.

Torpid yanked her down for a hug. "You have a family now, Mona."

Mona couldn't speak, but she squeezed Torpid

tighter and hid the tears that slipped from her eyes. A family.

"Come on," said Sandman, leading them back toward the doorway. "Let's leave them to it. Besides, we have a lot of work to do if you are going to learn how to become a Dream Weaver."

"About that," said Mona. "I have an idea."

26

A FEW MONTHS LATER...

he Sanctuary was alive with activity.

Kids ran through the corridors, stacks of books and papers in hand, ready for that night's classes.

Mona weaved between them all, wrapping her belt around her waist, the weight of the bags a heavy comfort to her now. The sand twinkled at her in anticipation. It was a big night for them, and for Mona. After weeks of practice, and long, frustrating nights conjuring, she was finally ready to try delivering her first-ever dream.

With the help of Sandman, of course. She still had a long way to go to complete her apprenticeship.

"Hey, Mona," said George, his baseball hat

Sanctuary requiring a bit of an upgrade now that it housed all the kids who couldn't find families back at Ms. Gloomberg's Home for Wayward Children. A whole extra level had been added, and it was only getting bigger as more and more kids arrived to learn the art of Dream Weaving.

"Hello, Mona," said Sandman when she arrived. "I was thinking we should make a stop at Kit's tonight. They've been thinking about us."

"Brilliant," said Mona. They hadn't seen Kit in three whole weeks due to the intense lessons Sandman had scheduled to get her ready for tonight. It would be nice to catch up.

"Are you ready?" He handed her a flask of warm hot chocolate for the journey.

Mona took a deep breath, anticipation dancing in her stomach. She reached for the chain around her neck and clutched her very own star-shaped vial filled with golden sand. "As ready as I'll ever be."

Sandman nodded. "Then let's be off."

And so, sand bags at the ready, the Sandman and his apprentice headed out to deliver dreams to everyone who needed them.

replaced with a floppy nightcap like the one Sandman always wore.

"Hey, George. How's the conjuring coming along?"

George sighed. "It's getting there. I almost made a rabbit the other day."

"Great," said Mona. "Keep practicing. You'll get the hang of it in no time."

A blond-headed girl ran past, but she tripped over her nightgown and toppled to the ground, the contents of her school bag spilling out over the floor.

George ran to help. "You okay, Ally?"

"Yeah, thanks, George," she said, gathering her things with him. "I wasn't paying attention to where I was going. You going to class?"

"You're both going to be late," said Mona. "Professor Torpid won't wait around for you to start his lesson."

While Torpid may not be able to use the sand himself, he had developed quite a skill in teaching the apprentices how to calm their minds to conjure what they wanted. He had certainly been a vital help for Mona when she was trying to bend the sand to her will down in the Land of Nightmares.

"Good luck tonight," said Ally, before she and George ran off toward the front of the ship.

Mona waved them goodbye and went to the kitchen. It took her longer than normal to reach, the